Introduction to the ANSYS
Design Language (APDL)

Second Edition

Compiled by:

The Tech Support Team at PADT, Inc.

Edited by:

Eric Miller

Phoenix Analysis & Design Technologies

7755 S Research Dr, Suite110

Tempe, AZ 85284

www.PADTINC.com

1-800-293-PADT

info@padtinc.com

ISBN: 1537133993

ISBN-13: 978-1537133997

Table of Contents

Chapter 1:   Introduction and APDL Overview

1.1   Introduction

The purpose of this document is to give an introduction into the ANSYS Parametric Design Language (APDL). You will learn why customization is important, what to customize, and to what level customization should be used. The reader will gain an understanding through the presentation of definitions, methods, usage instructions, and finally by applying it in workshops throughout the document.

1.2   Introduction to the Second Edition

We published this guide for the first time in 2013 with a bit of apprehension. Taking one of our training classes and turning it into a book seemed like a good idea when we started, but who knew if anyone would actually buy it. After three years we have sold over 600 copies to readers around the world. Not a best seller by any measure, but it shows that in the small community of ANSYS Mechanical and Mechanical APDL users, it is a valuable resource.

With the second edition we are making some updates, fixing typos and confusing passages that readers reported, and attempting to publish an e-book version. We also added two new sections; one on the APDL Math functions that have been added since the first edition was published and the second on how to include APDL code into your ANSYS Mechanical model.

But our purpose stays the same. We want to make this fantastically simple yet powerful scripting language called APDL available to more engineers.

1.3   Assumptions

This guide assumes that the user has a good understanding of the ANSYS Mechanical APDL product. Users should be beyond the "beginner" level of ANSYS usage. It also assumes that the user has access to a copy of ANSYS Mechanical APDL in order to work through the workshops provided.

ANSYS commands that are not part of APDL are not explained, so it is up to the reader to use the help manuals provided by ANSYS, Inc. with the software to look up and understand these commands.

In many places within the workshops you will notice that you are asked to enter in an equation rather than a number. This is to highlight the fact that ANSYS Mechanical APDL does calculations inside dialog boxes. Instead of doing the math in your head or in a spreadsheet, it is better to do it in the GUI or macro.

1.4   Workshop Files

Many of the workshops in this guide use files. You can find copies of the files in the Appendix 3. Information on how to download copies can also be found there.

1.5   Acknowledgements

This guide would have not been possible without decades of work by people at the company that is now ANSYS, Inc. Much of the material presented here is derived directly from manuals, training material, and examples produced by ANSYS, Inc.

It would also not have been possible without the generous contributions of many people in the ANSYS user community, who have shared their knowledge with other users. In particular, information from www.ANSYS.net was used heavily.

And lastly, we want to thank the developers of what is now called ANSYS Mechanical APDL, but that at one time was just ANSYS. We want to specifically thank the founder and original author, Dr. John Swanson. Not only did they create an extremely intuitive and powerful scripting tool, they shared their knowledge about APDL with PADT's employees throughout the years, and much of the "extra" information found within came from them.

1.6   APDL and ANSYS Mechanical

This guide is written for use with the ANSYS Mechanical APDL product. However, it can be used with ANSYS Mechanical through the addition of code to the model true. It is recommended that users try complicated macros out in ANSYS Mechanical APDL before using them in ANSYS Mechanical.

1.7   Overview Topics

The topics in this document include:

- APDL Macros
- Getting Started
- Parameters/Variables
- Interfacing with the User
- Program Flow in APDL
- Information Retrieval Topics
- Arrays and Tables
- Importing and Exporting Data to and from ANSYS
- Implementing Macros in a Group
- Tcl/Tk Use
- User Programmable Features (UPF)

- APDL Final Exam

1.8   Why Customize?

ANSYS Customization makes the analysis process *better, faster* and *cheaper*. ANSYS Customization is *better* because it automates and captures the analysis process, delivering better information that locks process into accepted practices, thus, avoiding inconsistency, it captures and distributes expertise, ensure repeatability, allows exploration of more design options, puts focus on goals rather than process, and, finally, allows attention to physics, not details. ANSYS Customization is *faster* because it greatly reduces cycle time by eliminating time spent "reinventing the wheel," removing repetitive and time consuming manual steps, reducing number of iterations needed to correct errors, lessening training and familiarization time, and reducing problems to key inputs and outputs. Finally, the process is *cheaper* due to cost savings realized beyond reduced cycle time and better analyses because training costs are lowered, fewer analysis experts are required, the software has better value, and it allows for more efficient use of in-house development staff.

Some of the other benefits of customization include more robust software, faster tool development times, portions of a given tool can be re-used, it makes bug tracking and fixing easier, adding functionality is easier and more robust, and it is easier for other people to understand.

1.9   What Level of Customization?

Customizing is an attractive feature for the reasons stated previous, it makes the analysis process better, faster and cheaper, but this is only true if customization is done well. There is a method that PADT recommends the reader follow in order to use customization properly. Planning the level of customization requires the user to:

1. Identify development & analysis goals
2. Separate geometry and topology
3. Use parameterization
4. Clearly understand current and proposed processes
5. Utilize Modularity
6. Allow batch, command line and GUI Interfaces
7. Crawl, Walk, Run

Identify Development & Analysis Goals

A common problem when customizing is focusing on the customization or analysis process and not on its goals. To prevent this, the user should ask questions such as:

Why are we doing this type of analysis?

What information are we looking for?

Who will use that information?

How detailed and accurate does the information need to be?

Who will use this tool?

How these questions are answered should be stored away and kept in mind as the customization tool is developed. On a larger project, it is even a good idea to print out a copy of these questions and their answers and place it somewhere in your workspace, as a reminder of where you are actually headed while you are nose deep in the weeds of creating your tools.

Separate Geometry and Topology

A common problem in tool design and implementation is confusing geometry and topology. *Geometry* is the size of various fundamental geometric entities like the length of a line, distance between holes, control polygon, and bounding curves on freeform surface. *Topology*, on the other hand, is how various fundamental geometric entities are connected to one another. For example, a 2D rectangle is made of four lines connected at right angles. Or a parallel-piped must have at least 6 distinct surfaces.

Figure 1-1 shows a simple example of how topology can be the same but geometry does not change, as well as an example of a topology change. The example on the left shows two areas that have the same topology, but the length of segment A and B have changed, creating different geometry. The example on the right shows that we have added two new segments, G and H. We also shortened segment F. So both the Topology and Geometry have changed.

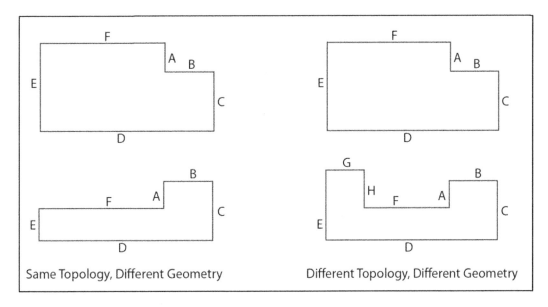

Figure 1.1: Differences between Geometry and Topology

This distinction is important because it is fairly simple to write an automation script that assumes constant topology. All that changes is the length and angle of components relative to one another. But when new entities are introduced into a geometric object, it is much more difficult to automate. Oftentimes when a macro that involves geometry breaks, it is because the topology that is assumed by the macro has changed. Once the author of the macro understands this, the macro can be made more general to allow for topology changes, or at least check for them and let the user know that topology has changed.

Use Parameterization

Using parameterization reduces problems to understandable fundamental inputs and outputs while capturing the design intent. For example, numerical parameters can drive geometry, "choice" parameters can drive topology, and output parameters can answer key design questions. Parameterization also enables optimization or design space exploration, aides in understanding and explaining system response, and results in faster tool development time and enables re-use of software.

Understand the Process

In almost all cases a macro is being written in APDL to automate some sort of process. Before that automation takes place it is very important to take the time and clearly understand the process. PADT recommends that all processes should be mapped out by identifying:

- The steps in the process, both the current process and the automated one
- Why each step is carried out
- The goal of each step or a group of steps
- The current and estimated cost for each step
- An estimate of the amount of time required to automate each step
- The level of quality required for each step

Process maps serve as road maps and cost/benefit checks during the development process by prompting the questions, 'Is it beneficial to automate a given step?' And 'How much time should be spent on automating a step?'

Flexibility

Interface flexibility allows a tool to be used in many ways. For example, as part of an optimization tool, a user created design space exploration, a variation study, and a module or call to a larger tool, as the starting point for a new tool. In addition, batch capability also speeds the development process by automatically verifying and debugging the runs. The user can use the GUI to become more familiar with the tool, but the command line or batch processes can be used for more efficiency.

Crawl, Walk, Run

The fundamental lesson that PADT has learned about ANSYS Customization is to start with a simple and easy automation of a beneficial process step and add complexity, user interface tools, and more process steps slowly. Finally, after establishing methods and benefits, implement the complete and user friendly automation of the process. The most common cause of failure is trying to do too much in the first release. So remember, Crawl, Walk, Run.

1.10 What to Customize

Table 1.1: Customization Level Examples shows a few case studies and recommendations when it comes to customization:

Case Studies	Recommendations
Case A: Simple Repeated Analysis from CAD Geometry imported from IGES Single loading condition	Create Macro to import geometry, apply BC's, and post-process. Do NOT add "user-friendly" features at this point
Case B: Weight Reduction Build geometry in ANSYS Update geometry to minimize weight given loading	Create Macro to build given topology, apply BC's and post-process. Do NOT add "user-friendly" features at this point.
Case C: Design Tool Design product as team Expect continuous improvement of design in future	Create Macro to define topology, build geometry, apply BC's and post-process. Add "user-friendly" features (prompts, menus, dialogs) as needed. Remember: CRAWL, WALK, RUN!

Table 1.1: Customization Level Examples

1.11 Definitions

Batch commands (command files) – Test commands valid at command line in the GUI, batch mode, or as an input file

Abbreviations – Text abbreviation for command(s); commonly added to the toolbar for frequent use

Macros – Text commands stored in a file and executed by an abbreviation, or read as an input file

APDL: ANSYS Parametric Design Language – a scripting language used to automate common tasks or even build your model in terms of parameters (variables). APDL includes batch commands as well as if-then-else branching, do-loops, and interfaces with the user.

GUI, The GUI – Refers to the graphical user interface that sits on top of the ANSYS Mechanical APDL program. The GUI is written in Tcl/Tk and is used to create the same APDL commands that users can type in. These commands are sent to the parser when executed.

1.12 The Command Interpreter

APDL is an interpreted language. It is not compiled into machine code and run at a low level. Each line in your program is read by a set of routines in the ANSYS Mechanical APDL program called the command interpreter. It reads the line and parses it as a command, a commented line, or information it needs for a previously executed command.

It is important to keep this in mind as you use APDL and especially as you debug your macros. Each line of code is executed as a command just as if you typed it into the ANSYS command line. In fact, you can cut and paste lines from your macro as a way to execute it one line at a time. Also remember that when you get an error, it is for the command being executed by the command interpreter.

1.13 What is a Macro?

Macros files are text command input files with the extension .mac and filename less than 32 characters long. Macros can have arguments passed to them when they are called and they can be called by the *USE command or the "unknown command" method.

Code example:

```
 *Use,mymacro,arg1,arg2 mymacro,arg1,arg2
 ! unknown commands such
 ! as "mymacro" are sought
! along the path defined by
! /psearch
```

1.14 Input files

Other text files, including those with the .mac extension, may be read in using the /INPUT,file,ext command or Utility Menu > File > Read input from...

The most common file extension for ANSYS input, besides .mac, is .inp. The .mac extension provides a quick shortcut to APDL file execution, since the file can be executed by typing the name ("name" in "name.mac") of the file in the command input window. However, .inp is frequently used for batch runs and one-time file execution.

1.15 Creating a macro

The following describes the four different methods that can be used to create an APDL macro.

Text Editor

Using a text editor is the preferred method because it allows you to work in an efficient way, keep a copy of what you are doing, and cut and paste from the editor window to the command window. There are many text editors available, both free and at a small cost. Using Notepad on windows or VI on Linux works just fine for occasional users. Users who spend a large amount of time writing macros should invest in a text editor that is context sensitive like PADT's PeDAL.

Probably the most commonly used text editor for making APDL macros is the text editor in ANSYS Mechanical that shows up in the worksheet when you edit a command stream.

Unless you need your macro to create a macro, this is the recommended way to create macros.

From a Macro using *CREATE

The *CREATE command is an old command. It takes a filename and extension as an argument (*CREATE,Fname,Ext) and it tells the command interpreter that all commands after the *CREATE command should not be interpreted, but instead write them to the file that was specified in the *CREATE. The command interpreter does this until it runs into the *END command.

Note that parameter names are not substituted when you use *CREATE.

The primary use for *CREATE is to generate batch input files for automatic execution. An example would be:

```
*create,run_ls_1to4,inp
resume,mymodel,db
/file,run_ls_1to4
save
/solu
lssolve,1,4
finish
*end
*create,run_ls_5to8,inp
resume,mymodel,db
/file,run_ls_5to8
save
/solu
```

```
lssolve,5,8
finish
*end
```

Another clever use for *CREATE is as a sort of macro library generator. If you are generating a set of tools that will have multiple macros that users can call, it is sometimes difficult managing access to all of those macros. So, instead of requiring a user to copy a large number of macros to a place where they can be executed, you create a single initializing macro that contains all the macros in one file bracketed by *create and *end for each macro. The user runs the creation macro, and all of the macros they need to call are created in the working directory.

*CFWRITE & *VWRITE

There are series of commands that can be used to open a file (*CFOPEN) write to it (*CFWRITE or *VWRITE) and close it (*CFCLOSE). These commands have two advantages over *CREATE. The first is that you can execute any APDL commands you want between a *CFOPEN and *CFCLOSE, information only gets written when you do a *CFWRITE or *VWRITE. The second is that parameter substitution takes place with *CFWRITE and *VWRITE so you can build macros or input files with the contents of parameters.

*VWRITE is covered in detail further in this guide because it is also used to write text files. The other three commands are very simple:

```
*CFOPEN,Fname,Ext,,Loc
! Fname: The filename. It can be just the root
!        (text before the .) or
!        the root and extension, or it can also include the directory
!        path.  248 characters max.
! Ext: The file extension if not provided in Fname
! Loc: Overwrite Flag
!       Blank:  Overwrite (Default)
!       APPEND: Append to an existing file.

*CFWRITE,Command
! Command: A string that will be written.
!          Any parameters in the string
!          will be evaluated. In addition, any functions
!          or math operations will also be evaluated and the
 !           results will be written to the file
*CFCLOSE
```

External Program or Programming Language

A very common method used by power users to create macros is to use an external program. Users employ python, C++, or even Microsoft Excel to write out APDL commands into a file. Some users will use the programming language found in other simulation tools to create APDL scripts as well. There really is no limit because APDL is a simple command driven text based language.

1.16   Entities and Numbering in ANSYS Mechanical APDL

One very key concept that pervades almost every aspect of ANSYS Mechanical APDL is the fact that everything in your model is considered an entity by the program and it has a number. If you work in the GUI all the time you never really have to worry about the entity numbering, but if you are writing macros then entity numbering is everything.

When you create most entities, the program assigns an entity number. But with many of the entity types you can specify what number you want. You use APDL commands to find out what entity numbers are, and use parameters and do-loops to step through entities. Most users who approach come to APDL through ANSYS Mechanical or from only using a GUI do not pay enough attention to the basic concept of entity numbers. Almost all engineering software tools use numbering internally. Understanding and leveraging this can offer significant advantages in APDL.

Chapter 2:   Getting Started

2.1   Introduction

In this chapter we will go over some very basic aspects of APDL – namely commands, help, and how to execute commands. Even if you are an old ANSYS pro, do not skip this chapter because it builds some important concepts. It is especially important that you work through the workshop as shown because you will need to use the macro you create for future workshops.

2.2   ANSYS Commands

Every command in the ANSYS Mechanical APDL menus has a text command equivalent. Some examples are shown in the table below.

Menu Pick	Command Equivalent
Preprocessor> Create> Sphere> Solid Sphere> WP X = 0 WP Y = 0 Radius = 1	SPH4,,,1
Solution> Apply> Other> Angular Velocity> OMEGX = 0 OMEGY = 100 OMEGZ = 0	OMEGA,,100,
General Postproc> Plot Results> Nodal Solution DOF Solution Translation UX	PLNSOL,U,X
Utility Menu> List> Loads> DOF Constraints> On All Nodes	DOFSEL,S,UX,DLIST

Table 2.1: Example Menu Picks and their APDL Equivilent

Command Syntax

The command syntax is as follows: `Command, arg1, arg2, arg3, arg4...`

Command equivalents appear in all caps and enclosed in square brackets in dialog windows or the user prompt area of the GUI window.

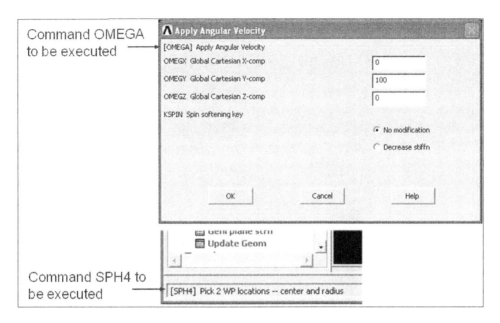

Figure 2.1: Command Name in Dialog Box

Executing Commands

Commands can be executed by:

1. Typing at the GUI's command line

Figure 2.2: GUI Command Line

2. Typing at the command line in Command-Line Mode

3. Reading from external text file (in GUI or Batch mode)

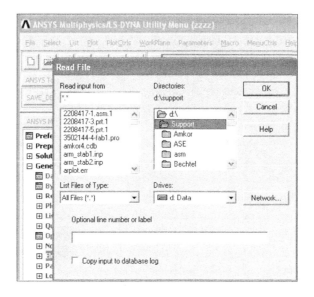

Figure 2.3: Reading an Input File with the GUI

2.3   Commenting

As with any language, it is very important to use comments liberally in your macros so that everyone, including you, can figure out what is going on and why you did things the way you did.

There are two ways to comment in APDL:

The first method uses the /COM command:

```
/COM, This is a comment, it can be up to 80 characters long
```

Although this is an older method and a bit more typing, it has the advantage of echoing whatever you put as the comment to the output file. So it is not just a comment, it also is a way to write out information to your output stream.

The second and more common method is to place an exclamation point at the start of the characters you want for your comment. Everything to the right of, and including the exclamation point is ignored by the command parser, even more exclamation points and quotes. Figure 2.4 shows some good examples.

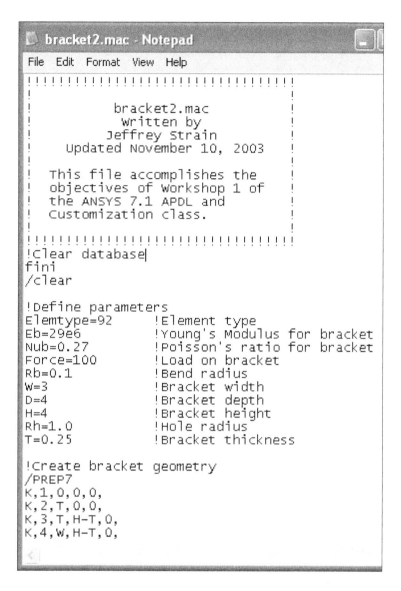

Figure 2.5: Examples of Commenting with !

2.4   Accessing Help for Commands

Users can get assistance with commands in several different ways. If the GUI is being used and dialog boxes are open, there is usually a "Help" button in the dialog box. Pressing that button will bring up help for that specific command.

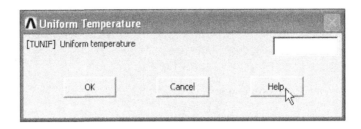

Figure 2.6: Help Button

You can also access help files from the menu: Utility Menu> Help> Help Topics>

The fastest way to get help on a specific command is to simply type in HELP, *command*. That will bring up the help page for that particular command.

2.5   Log Files

The file Jobname.LOG opens when you enter the ANSYS program and records all the commands typed or executed via menu picks. Use the log file to repeat commands or edit and rename the log file and read it as an input file.

```
Λ Log File                                                                    X
File
/BATCH                                                                         ^
/COM,ANSYS RELEASE  7.1    UP20030501        10:00:52    11/07/2003
/input,menust,tmp,'',,,,,,,,,,,,,,,,1
/GRA,POWER
/GST,ON
/PLO,INFO,3
/GRO,CURL,ON
/CPLANE,1
WPSTYLE,,,,,,,,0
/REPLOT,RESIZE
/PREP7
k
kplot,,,,,,,,,1
k,,1,1,,1
kplot,,,,,,,,,1
1,1,2
FLST,5,1,4,ORDE,1
FITEM,5,1
lsel, , , ,P51X
!*
lprojmen
/VIEW,1,1,1,1
/ANG,1
/REP,FAST
lplo                                                                          v
```

Figure 2.7: Log File Example

The log file is a way to build macros in a semi-automatic way. Simply use the GUI to go through the process you want to automate, then save the resulting log file and edit it for more general use. This is especially recommended for newer users or users who are using a part of the program they are not familiar with.

2.6   Workshop 1: Getting Started

In this workshop you will use menu picks to build the illustrated geometry. After meshing and applying loads, you will then use the Log File to create an editable input file which creates the geometry and mesh, and applies BC's. You will also make changes to the input file, including a change to the hole size – this demonstrates the flexibility afforded by an input file rather than using only menu picks.

Workshop 1 Setup:

Create an 'L'-shaped bracket with the following characteristics:

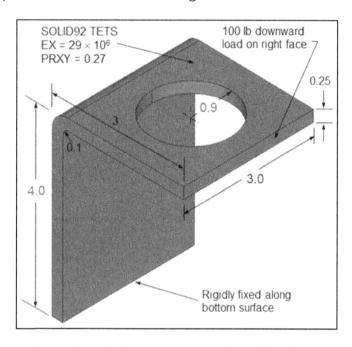

Figure 2.8: Workshop 1 Geometry and Model Definition

When performing this exercise, note the ANSYS commands given in the command window when a menu command is executed. Also consider design intent throughout the exercise.

Workshop Procedure

While going through this Workshop, you might do something that you would like to undo. ANSYS MAPDL does not have an 'undo' button, but there is a way to remove commands that were generated and rebuild the model from there. The steps are:

- Click on Session Editor under the ANSYS Main Menu
- Delete the offending command
- Click save
- Click OK and the model should be rebuilt

1: Define jobname as "bracket"

2: File > Change Jobname

3: Enter "bracket" for the jobname

4: Create keypoints to define corners of area to be extruded

Preprocessor > Modeling > Create > Keypoints > In Active CS

Enter the following X,Y,Z values as shown for keypoint locations:

- NPT 1: 0, 0, 0   (Click 'Apply')
- NPT 2: 0.25, 0, 0   (Click 'Apply')
- NPT 3: 0.25, 4-0.25, 0   (Click 'Apply')
- NPT 4: 3, 4-0.25, 0   (Click 'Apply')
- NPT 5: 3, 4, 0   (Click 'Apply')
- NPT 6: 0, 4, 0   (Click 'OK')

Your screen should look like the following image. Please note that keypoints 1 and 2 are located very close to the coordinate system x, y, and z markers which can make them difficult to see. For Step 3 below, you'll need to hover your mouse over the points near the coordinate marker in order to select them.

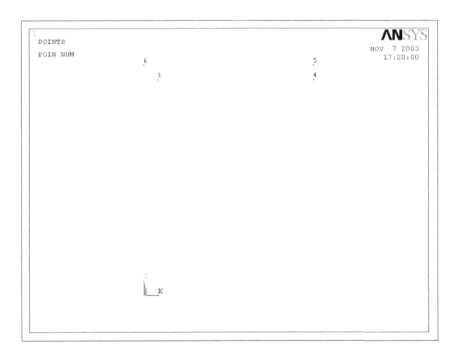

Figure 2.9: Workshop 1 results after steps 1 and 2

5: Create lines between keypoints 3 and 6 and their adjacent keypoints

Preprocessor > Modeling > Create > Lines > Lines > In Active Coord

Connect the following keypoints:

- 1 and 6, 6 and 5, 2 and 3, 3 and 4

6: Turn on Line Numbers and Keypoint Numbers and Create fillets from lines 1 to 2 and 3 to 4

Utility Menu > PlotCtrls > Numbering > Line Numbers, On > OK
or: /pnum,line,1

Utility Menu > PlotCtrls > Numbering > Keypoint Numbers, On > OK
or: /pnum,kp,1

Utility Menu > Plot > LInes

Preprocessor > Modeling > Create > Lines > Line Fillet

- Pick lines 1 and 2

- Click Apply

- Enter a radius of 0.1+0.25 in the popup box

- Click Apply

- Pick lines 3 and 4

- Click Apply

- Enter a radius of 0.1 in the popup box

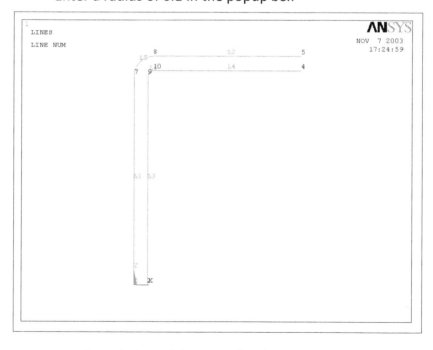

Figure 2.10: Workshop 1 results after steps 5 and 6

7: Create an area through all keypoints

Preprocessor > Modeling > Create > Areas > Arbitrary > Through KPs

     - Pick keypoints 1, 2, 9, 10, 4, 5, 8, and 7, in that order

     - Click OK

8: Extrude the area 3 inches

Preprocessor > Modeling > Operate > Extrude > Areas > By XYZ Offset

     - Select the area

     - Click apply

     - Enter a value of 3 for DZ in the popup window

     - Click OK

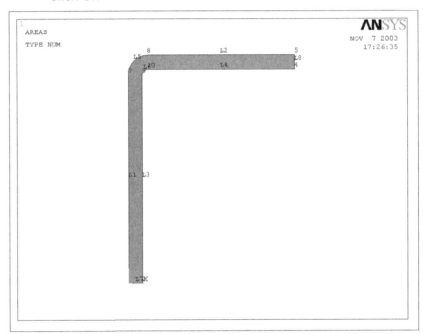

Figure 2.11: Workshop 1 results after steps 7 and 8

9: Now you need to align the WorkPlane with center of top area to create a through-hole. First, the WorkPlane must be offset to the center of the area. Then, it must be rotated so that it is parallel with the area

Adjust to the Isometric view using the ISO button on the right hand side of the GUI:

Then click the fit to screen button:

Utility Menu > WorkPlane > Offset WP to > Keypoints

     - Pick keypoints 5 and 17 (or 16 and 8)

     - Click OK

Utility Menu > WorkPlane > Offset WP by Increments

- In the "Offset WP" Tool, enter values of 0,-90,0 below "XY,YZ,ZX Angles."

- Click OK

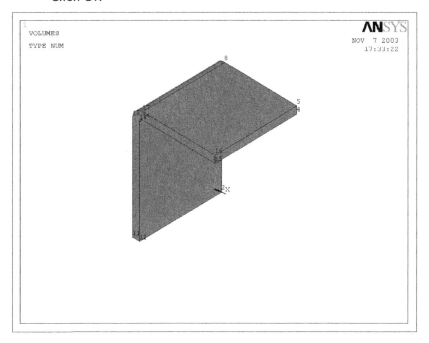

Figure 2.12: Workshop 1 results after step 9

10: Create cylinder to be subtracted from volume

Preprocessor > Modeling > Create > Volumes > Cylinder > Solid Cylinder

- In the dialog box, leave WP X and WP Y blank

- Enter a value of 0.90 for Radius and -0.25 for Depth. Make sure to include the negative sign for the depth

- Click OK

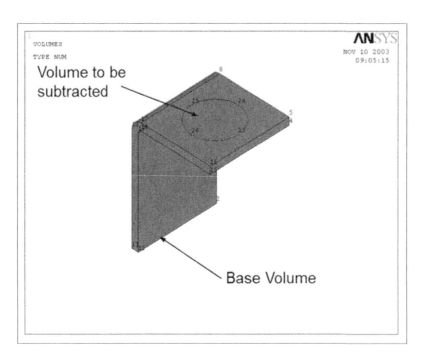

Figure 2.13: Workshop 1 results after steps 10 and 11

11: Subtract cylinder from volume

Preprocessor > Modeling > Operate > Booleans > Subtract > Volumes

- Pick the 'L'-shaped volume as the base volume from which to subtract
- Click OK
- Select the cylinder as the volume to be subtracted
- Click OK

12: Define element type

Preprocessor > Element Type > Add/Edit/Delete

- Click the "Add" button and select "Structural Solid" and "Tet 10node 187"

13: Define material properties

Preprocessor > Material Props > Material Models > Structural > Linear > Elastic > Isotropic

- Enter 29E6 for EX and 0.27 for PRXY

14: Define the element size such that there are 2 divisions across the thickness.

Open the MeshTool box by selecting *Preprocessor > Meshing > MeshTool*

Beneath "Size Controls" next to "Global" click the "Set" button

- Enter a value of 0.25/2 for SIZE

15: Mesh the volume

In the MeshTool box:

- Verify that "Volumes" is selected next to "Mesh"
- Verify that "Tet" is selected next to "Shape"
- Click the "Mesh" button and "Pick All."

16: Enter the Solution Processor.

Main Menu > Solution

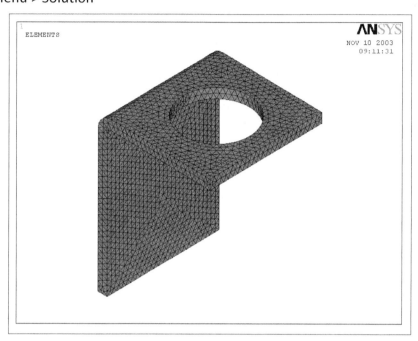

Figure 2.14: Workshop 1 results after step 16

17: Constrain the bottom surface

Solution > Define Loads > Apply > Structural > Displacement > On Areas

- Select the bottom area and "OK"
- Select "All DOF" and "OK"

18: Select the area to which the downward force is to be applied

Utility Menu > Select > Entities

- Select "Areas," "By Num/Pick,"
- "From Full" and click "Apply"
- Select the area on the right face of the bracket and "OK"

19: Select the nodes attached to the area selected in step 18 (the Select Entities window should already be open, but sometimes it can get hidden by other windows, so just filter through until you locate it)

Select "Nodes," "Attached to," "Areas, all," "From Full" and click "OK"

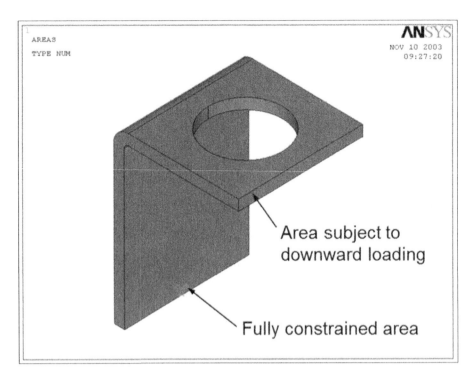

Figure 2.15: Workshop 1 results after step 19

20: Create a parameter, NUMNODE, equal to the number of selected nodes

Utility Menu > Parameters > Get Scalar Data > Model data, For selected set

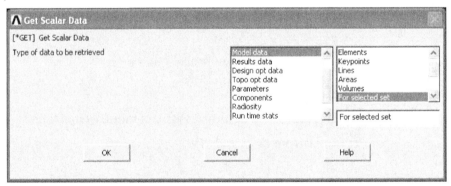

In the next dialog window, type NUMNODE next to Name of parameter to be defined and select Current node set, No. of Nodes

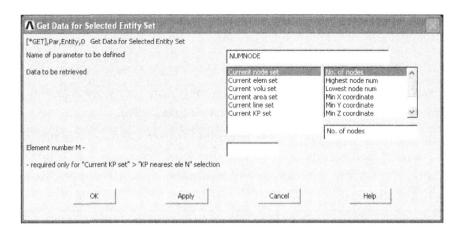

21: Apply a downward force of 100 lbs to the selected nodes

Solution > Define Loads > Apply > Structural > Force/Moment > On Nodes > [Pick All]

- Select "FY" and enter a value of -100/NUMNODE (it is normal to receive a warning message, simply close it)

22: Select all entities: Utility Menu > Select > Everything

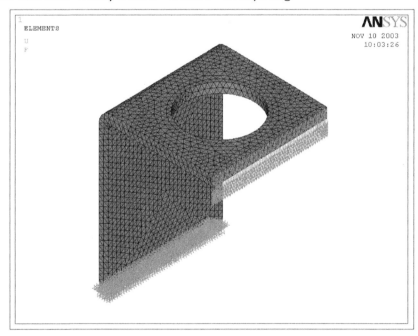

Figure 2.16: Workshop 1 results after step 23

23: Transfer the loads to the mesh (this is also done automatically when a solve command is issued).

Solution > Define Loads > Operate > Transfer to FE > All Solid Lds

24: Exit ANSYS and save the model

Toolbar > QUIT

- Select "Save Geom+Loads"

- click "OK"

25: Review and edit the log file

In Windows Explorer or another file management tool, copy bracket.log to bracket1.mac and then open bracket1.mac in a text editor.

Edit as shown in the following figures. Also feel free to clean up the file to improve the presentation eliminating plot commands (aplot, vplot, etc.), graphics commands (/view, /ang, /replot, etc.) and any other commands that are not necessary to creating the model:

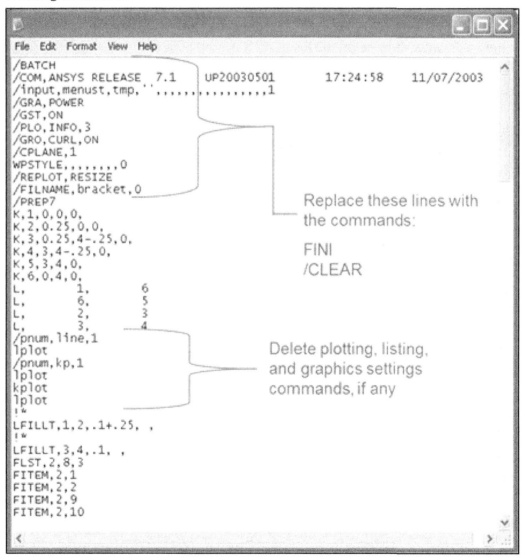

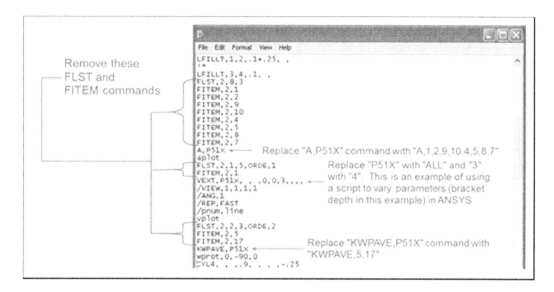

Remove these FLST and FITEM commands

Replace "A,P51X" command with "A,1,2,9,10,4,5,8,7"

Replace "P51X" with "ALL" and "3" with "4". This is an example of using a script to vary parameters (bracket depth in this example) in ANSYS

Replace "KWPAVE,P51X" command with "KWPAVE,5,17"

Note: Although not necessary for this example, the FLST and FITEM commands can be useful when the order of entities is important and the number of arguments for a command is limited. See Help for more information.

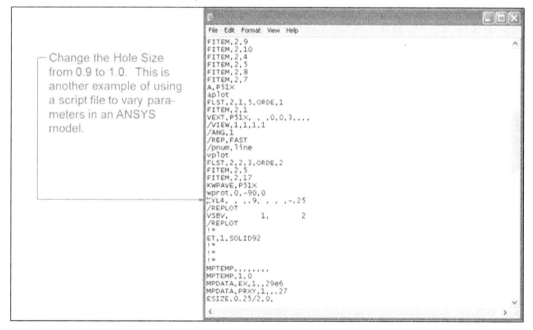

Change the Hole Size from 0.9 to 1.0. This is another example of using a script file to vary parameters in an ANSYS model.

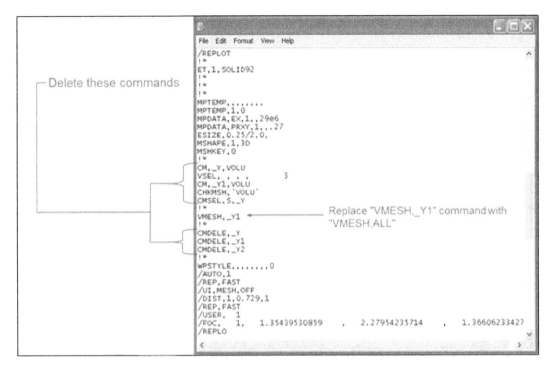

Delete these commands

Replace "VMESH,_Y1" command with "VMESH,ALL"

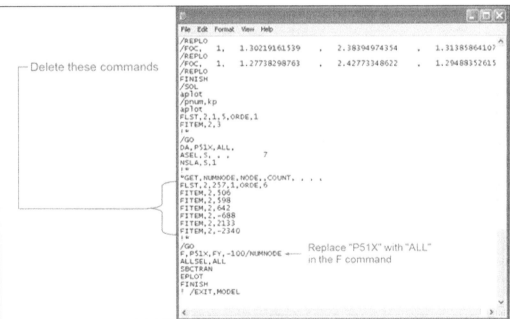

Delete these commands

Replace "P51X" with "ALL" in the F command

26: Now it is time to run your newly created macro

Save the file and exit the text editor

Start ANSYS using the jobname bracket1

Input the file bracket1.mac by typing bracket1 in the command input window

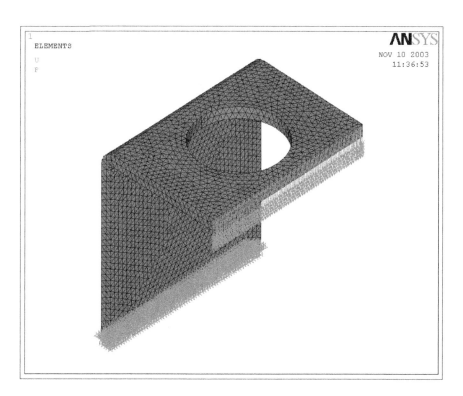

Figure 2.17: Completed Model from Workshop 1

END OF WORKSHOP

Chapter 3: Parameters

3.1 Introduction

One of the key capabilities that makes APDL an actual programming language instead of just a list of commands is its support of variables. Variables are called parameters in APDL and they come in many shapes and sizes. It is very important that you understand all those options and how they work, especially how substitution works, so that you can expose the full power of APDL.

3.2 Defining a Scalar Parameter

To define a scalar parameter (variable), use the following format:

```
NAME = VALUE
```

NAME is the parameter name – eight alphanumeric characters or less.

VALUE may be a number, a previously defined parameter, a mathematical function, a parametric expression, or a character string.

This can be placed in a macro or typed in to the command line.

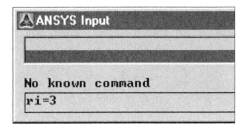

Figure 3.1: Example of Defining a Scalar Parameter on the Command Line

Or you can use the GUI's scalar parameters dialog (Utility menu > Parameters > Scalar Parameters ...):

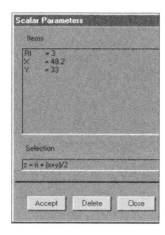

Figure 3.2: Defining a Scalar Parameter using the GUI

The following is a list of typical parameter definitions that one might use in a macro. Note that some include inline mathematical operations and others use functions.

```
inrad=2.5              g=386                    bb=cos(30)
outrad=8.2             massdens=density/g       pi=acos(-1)
numholes=4             circumf=2*pi*rad         slope=(y2-y1)/(x2-x1)
thick=outrad-inrad     area=pi*r**2             theta=atan(slope)
e=2.7e6                                         jobname='proj1'
                       dist=sqrt((y2-
density=0.283            y1)**2+(x2-x1)**2)
```

Another way to define a scalar value, and the original way that is more consistent with the standard APDL syntax, is to use the *SET command.

```
*SET, NAME, VALUE
```

Example:

```
*SET,inrad,2.5
```

3.3 Global and Local Parameters

Most parameters in APDL are global. Once you or the ANSYS program itself defines a parameter, it exists until you delete it or clear the database. When you save a database to a *.db file, the parameters are written to that file and are available when you resume. They are also stored in a *.CDB file if you archive your model.

The exception to this are parameters ARG1-ARG9 and AR10-AR99. These are local to the macro they are created in, simply because ANSYS deletes ARG1-ARG99 when a macro is done running. The most common way that these are defined is when you call a macro and pass it an argument. ARG1-ARG9 and AR10-AR19 are defined this way. If you want to create local variables that just stays in your macro, you can use AR20-AR99.

3.4   Deleting Parameters

Because parameters are global and never go away, you should always clean up parameters when you are done with them or they will clutter up your database. The easiest way to delete a parameter is to set it to nothing:

```
myParam =
```

You can also use the *DEL command:

```
*DEL,Val1,Val2
! VAL1:
!     ALL: Delete all parameters, user defined and/or system defined.
!     Blank: use Val2 to specify which parameters to delete
! VAL2:
!     LOC:  Used by the GUI mostly. LOC is the position in the
!           Array Parameter Dialog box.
!    _PRM:  If VAL1 = ALL, deletes all parameters including those that
!           start with an underscore.  These are usually
!            system parameters
!           If Val1 = Blank, then just delete parameters that start
!                    with an underscore
!    PRM_: Delete parameters that end in an underscore.
!          Does not work with Val1 = ALL
!   Blank: If Val1 is blank, delete all user defined parameters and
!          leave any with a leading or trailing underscore alone.
```

Looking at these options it becomes obvious that you should never have a macro that does a *DEL,ALL,_PRM. It will wipe out all the parameters, including those you defined and system parameters. In fact, it is never recommended to do a *DEL,,_PRM as well because you never know what parameters the program itself needs.

If you create your parameters with a trailing underscore, it makes it very easy to clean up when your macro is done with a *DEL,,PRM_. If you did not use this convention, then it is a very good idea to delete the parameters one at a time that were only needed by your macro to keep the database clean and not provide any unknown "default" values to downstream programs.

3.5   Array Parameters

ANSYS also supports *array* parameters, which have multiple values. Both numeric and character arrays are available as well as tables. Arrays and tables will be covered later.

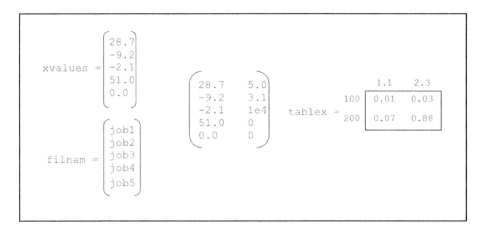

Figure 3.3: Examples of Array Parameters

3.6 Naming rules

The following rules apply to parameter names:

- Parameter names must be 32 characters or less, beginning with a letter.
  - o As a side note: Versions 5.7.1 and earlier limit the number of characters to eight or less. This is why some older scripts, and older users, will have very short names.
- Only letters, numbers, and the underscore character are allowed.
- Avoid underscore as starting character. ANSYS uses it to name internal parameters so if you do not use it, you will avoid overwriting the internal values.
- Consider ending parameters names with underscore.
  - o When you list parameters, by default those ending in underscore do not list. This is a way to hide parameters from users
  - o You can also delete all your parameters in one command if you use the trailing underscore with `*DEL,,PRM_`.
- Names are *not* case-sensitive, e.g., "RAD" and "Rad" are the same. All parameters are internally stored in capital letters.
- Avoid common ANSYS labels such as EX, STAT, DEFA, and ALL.
- ARG1 through AR99 have specific uses in macros as we will see later.

To use a parameter, simply enter its name in the appropriate field in the dialog box or on the command. For example, we define a rectangle using the parameters w=10 and h=5.

Using the GUI:

Utility menu > Parameters > Scalar Parameters ...

- Enter: w = 10
- Enter h = 5
- Click Accept

Preprocessor > Modeling > Create >
Areas > Rectangle > By 2 Corners

- Enter the characters w and h for height and width

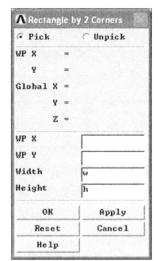

**Figure 3.4: GUI Definition
of Rectangle using
Parameters**

Using commands:

```
/prep7
w = 10
h = 5
Blc4,,,w,h
```

ANSYS immediately substitutes parameter values. The rectangle in the above example is stored as a 10 x 5 area, not as w x h. If the value of w or h changes after creating the rectangle, the area will NOT update.

Here are some other examples of using parameters:

```
jobname='proj1'
/filnam,jobname    ! Jobname

/prep7
youngs=30e6
mp,ex,1,youngs     ! Young's modulus

force=500
fk,2,fy,-force            ! Force at KP 2
fk,6,fx,force/2           ! Force at KP 6
```

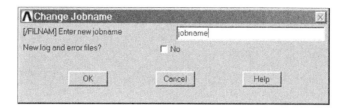

Figure 3.5: GUI Parameter Substitution - Jobname

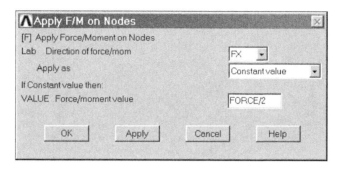

Figure 3.6: GUI Parameter Substitution - Forces

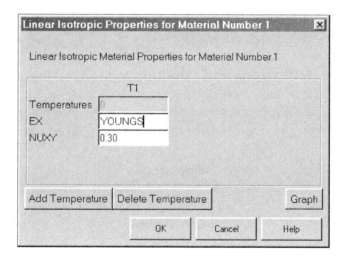

Figure 3.7: GUI Parameter Substitution - Material Properties

3.7   Listing Parameters

As with all things you can create in ANSYS Mechanical APDL, you can list parameters. The command is a little different than most listing commands though. Use *STATUS to list out parameters of all types, using the arguments for the command to control what is listed and how it is listed.

```
*STATUS, Par,IMIN,IMAX,JMIN,JMAX,KMIN,KMAX,LMIN,LMAX,MMIN,MMAX,KPRI
! Par: Determines which parameters or types of parameters are written
!      ALL or blank: List all parameters and toolbar abbreviations
!                    except those with leading or trailing underscores
!      _PRM, PRM_: List parameters with leading (_PRM) or trailing
```

```
!               (PRM_) underscores in their names
!       ABBR: List toolbar abbreviations (not really applicable to
!             APDL programming)
!       PARM: List all parameters except those with leading or
!             trailing underscores
!       MATH: List APDL Math parameters (not covered in this guide)
!       parname: A parameters name, only list that parameter
!       argx: List all parameters supplied as arguments to the
!             macro being run (ARG1-ARG99)
! IMIN,IMAX,JMIN,JMAX,KMIN,KMAX,LMIN,LMAX,MMIN,MMAX:
!             Min and max values for array indices.  Use to list only
!             portions of an array.
! KPRI: Flag to control listing of labels for Tables
!             1: List labels, (default)
!             0: Do not list labels
```

Array parameters list differently than scalar ones. If you use ALL, blank, PARM, or PRM_, then the program just lists that names and flags them as being arrays. To see the contents, you must give the array name as the first argument. If you want to control how much of the array is written, use the xMIN/xMax arguments.

3.8   Parametric Operations and Functions

Parametric operations and functions manipulate variables with ANSYS-defined operators and functions. The following is a complete listing of available operators and functions:

Operators	
+	Addition
-	Subtraction
*	Multiplication
/	Division
**	Exponentiation

Table 3.1: Operators in APDL

Function	Description
ABS(x)	Absolute Value
SIGN(x,y)	Absolute value of x with sign of y
CXABS(x,y)	Absolute value of complex number x + yi
EXP(x)	Exponential of x
LOG(x)	Natural log of x
LOG10(x)	Common log of x
SQRT(x)	Square root of x
NINT(x)	Nearest integer to x
MOD(x,y)	Remainder of x/y
RAND(x,y)	Random number between x and y
GDIS(x,y)	Random number by Gaussian distribution with mean x and standard deviation y
SIN(x), COS(x), TAN(x)	Sine, Cosine, and Tangent of x
SINH(x), COSH(x), TANH(x)	Hyperbolic Sine, Cosine, and Tangent of x
ASIN(x), ACOS(x), ATAN(x)	Arcsine, Arccosine, and Arctangent of x
ATAN2(y,x)	Arctangent of y/x
VALCHR (CPARM)	Numerical value of string CPARM
CHRVAL (PARM)	Turns number PARM into a string
UPCASE (CPARM)	Converts CPARM into all upper case letters
LWCASE (CPARM)	Converts CPARM into all lower case letters
IBSET(b1,n2)	Set the n2 bit in value b1
IBCLR(b1,n2)	Clear the n2 bit in value b1
BTEST(b1,n2)	Test the n2 bit in the value b1 (return 1.0 if bit is set)
BITAND(b1,b2)	Bitwise AND of b1 and b2
BITOR(b1,b2)	Bitwise OR of value b1 and b2
BITXOR(b1,b2)	Bitwise XOR of value b1 and b2
BITSET(b1,b2)	Use b2 as a mask to set bits in b1
BITCLEAR(b1,b2)	Use b2 as a mask to clear bits in b1

Table 3.2: Parametric Functions in APDL

Additional information on additional string functions can be found in Chapter 7.

3.9   Units for Trigonometric Functions

By default, the angles used in trig functions are assumed to be in radians. The angle units can be changed to degrees by executing `*AFUN,  DEG` or using the GUI command Utility Menu > Parameters > Angular Units.

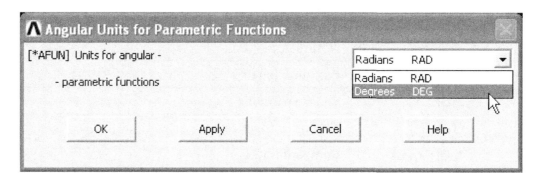

Table 3.3: Dialog Box for Changing Angular Units

3.10   Saving/Restoring Parameters

You can write and read all parameters to a file. This aids documentation, transferring data between databases, or restoring previous data sets. This can also be particularly handy when you are hooking up ANSYS Mechanical APDL to an optimization tool.

To write parameters to a file, use PARSAV:

```
PARSAV, Lab, Fname, Ext
! Lab
!         SCALAR: write only scalar parameters (default)
!          ALL: write all scalar and array parameters
! Fname
!         Filename and directory path
! Ext
!         Filename extension. Default is blank
```

To read in a file that you created with PARSAV, use PARRES

```
PARRES, Lab, Fname, Ext
! Lab
!         NEW: Deletes all existing parameters and replaces them with
!              parameters in the file (default)
!          CHANGE: Adds new parameters and changes existing ones
! Fname
!         Filename and directory path
! Ext
!         Filename extension. Default is blank
```

Sometimes you want to just read and write one or a couple of parameters. To do that you use the *VWRITE and *VREAD commands. This will be covered later in detail.

- To write parameters to file, use: PARSAV –list commands
- To read parameters from file use: PARRES
- To write/read selected parameters (covered later) use: *VWRITE and *VREAD

3.11   Using Parameters in Commands

Most commands in ANSYS that take a number or a string as an argument will automatically convert a parameter into the value it holds. As an example:

```
x1 = 12.5
y1 = 14.5
z1 = 1.3
n,x1,y1,z1
! Makes node at (12.5,14.5,1.3)
```

The help will tell you if the argument can be a parameter or a value.

Sometimes, you need to tell the command interpreter that you have a parameter and you want it to substitute its value in instead of its name. You do this by putting the parameter name inside two percent signs. The most common usages are imbedding values in a character string or specifying a table parameter for a load.

```
MyName = 'Edwardo'
/title, Analysis created by %MyName%
*DIM,SYCNV,TABLE,3,3,,RPM,TEMP

SYCNV(1,0)=0.0,20.0,40.0
SYCNV(0,1)=0.0,10.0,20.0,40.0
SYCNV(0,2)=0.5,15.0,30.0,60.0
SYCNV(0,3)=1.0,20.0,40.0,80.0
SF,ALL,CONV,%SYCNV%
```

3.12   Workshop 2: Building Parametric Models

In this workshop you will modify the bracket1.mac file to define the dimensions and material properties in terms of parameters. Use the values from Workshop 1 as default values for the parameters in Workshop 2.

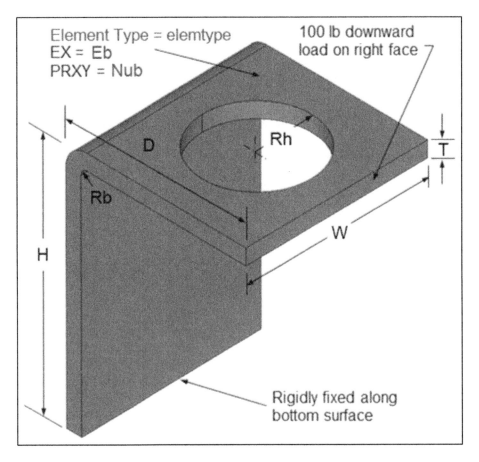

Figure 3.8: Workshop 2 Model, Values and Parameters

While going through this Workshop, you might do something that would be similar to undo. ANSYS MAPDL does not have an 'undo' button, but there is a way to remove commands that were generated and rebuild the model from there. The steps are:

Click on Session Editor under the ANSYS Main Menu

Delete the offending command>click save>click OK and the model should be rebuilt

1: Begin by opening bracket1.mac and adding these variables to the start of the macro after the /CLEAR command.

```
Elemtype = 187
Eb = 29e6
Nub = 0.27
Force = 100
Rb = 0.1
W = 3
D = 3
H = 4
Rh = 1.0
```

```
T = 0.25
```

2: Modify the following lines as shown. The first line of each pair shows what is in the file, and the second is what you want to change it to:

```
K,2,.25,0,0
K,2,T,0,0

K,3,0.25,4-.25,0,
K,3,T,H-T,0,

K,4,3,4-.25,0,
K,4,W,H-T,0,

K,5,3,4,0,
K,5,W, H,0,

K,6,0,4,0,
K,6,0,H,0,

LFILLT,1,2,0.1+.25, ,
LFILLT,1,2,Rb+T, ,

LFILLT,3,4,0.1, ,
LFILLT,3,4,Rb, ,

VEXT,ALL, , ,0,0,4,,,,
VEXT,ALL, , ,0,0,D,,,,

CYL4,,,1,,,,-.25
CYL4,,,Rh,,,,-T

ET,1,SOLID92
ET,1,elemtype

MPDATA,EX,1, ,29e6,
MPDATA,EX,1, ,Eb

MPDATA,PRXY,1, ,.27,
MPDATA,PRXY,1 , ,nub,

ESIZE,.25/2,0,
ESIZE,T/2,0,

F,ALL,FY,-100/numnode
F,ALL,FY,-force/numnode
```

3: Now it is time to run you parameterized macro

Save the file as bracket2.mac

Input the file bracket2.mac by typing bracket2 in the command input window

Debug bracket2.mac if necessary

4: The next thing you want to do is actually change parameters. Since we are not running the model the only thing that you will be able to see are changes to the geometry.

Edit the bracket2.mac by changing T to 0.35 and W to 5

Input the modified file and view the results

END OF WORKSHOP

Chapter 4:   Interfacing with the User

4.1   Introduction

In many cases you will be writing macros for yourself or that will be run in batch mode. In those cases, just opening up the macro file and changing parameter values will be good enough. But sometimes you can see significant productivity gains by interacting with the user and prompting them to set parameters or displaying information. In this chapter we will cover how to do both.

4.2   Prompting the User

You can prompt the user for an input value with *ASK. This is the simplest and easiest way to prompt for a variable. But it is also the most annoying if you need multiple variables, so use it with care and use MULTIPRO, discussed in the next session, if you have more than one or two parameters you need to prompt for at a time.

This command is formatted as follows:

```
*ASK,PAR,Query,DVAL
      ! PAR:parameter name to store value
      ! QUERY: prompt message up to 54 characters long
      ! DVAL: default value to use
```

An example of the command is:

```
*ASK, crsleng,the length of this course,72
```

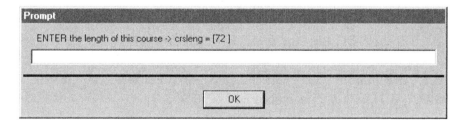

Figure 4.1: Example of *ASK Dialog

Note that the command prepends the string supplied as the QUERY argument with ENTER.

4.3   MULTIPRO Command

To prompt the User for multiple input values, use the MULTIPRO command. MULTIPRO is itself a macro, so the format of the command and the options you use with it are a bit unusual. But once you get the hang of it you can very quickly and easily prompt for parameters.

There are two commands that one uses to make a MULTIPRO dialog: MULTIPRO and *CSET.

```
MULTIPRO,Lab,Prompt_Num
    ! Lab: Flags the macro if you are starting or ending a prompt.
    !      Value must be in single quotes.
    !      'start': Enter to begin a multipro definition
    !      'end': Enter to finish a multipro definition
    ! Prompt_Num: The number of parameters you will be prompting for
    !             Not required unless you do not specify a default value
    !             for any of the parameters


*CSET,Strt_Loc,End_Loc,Param_Name,'Prompt_String',Def_Value
    ! Strt_Loc, End_Loc: Start and end value for information for this
    !                    parameter.  End_Loc is always Start_loc+2.
    !                    Think of the dialog box as a table:
    !                       1[Prompt1]   2[PARAM1]    3[VALUE1]
    !                       4[Prompt1]   5[PARAM1]    6[VALUE1]
    !                       7[Prompt1]   8[PARAM1]    9[VALUE1]
    !                    See figure below.
    ! Param_Name: The name of the parameter you want the user to define
    ! 'Prompt_String': A string, in single quotes, to prompt the
    !                    user with. 32 character max.
    ! Def_Value: A default value. It can be an APDL parameter. If left
    !            blank, the current value of Param_Name will be used.
```

In addition to the parameter prompts there are two saved rows at the top of the dialog box that contain two 32-character strings each: 61,62 and 63,64.

When multipro,'end' is executed, the dialog box pops up on the screen for the user.

When the user clicks on OK, the macro takes the parameters you provided and set them to the values the user entered. It also sets the internal parameter _BUTTON to 0. If they clicked CANCEL, then it does not assign any values to parameters and it sets _BUTTON to 1. Always check _BUTTON in your macro.

Here is a simple example:

```
multipro,'start',3
    *cset,1,3,beamW,'Enter beam width',12.5
    *cset,4,6,beamH,'Enter beam height',23.345
    *cset,7,9,beamL,'Enter beam length',50.0
    *cset,61,62,'Input the Sizes of',' The dimensions that'
    *cset,63,64,'are specified below',' and Have Fun!'
multipro,'end'
```

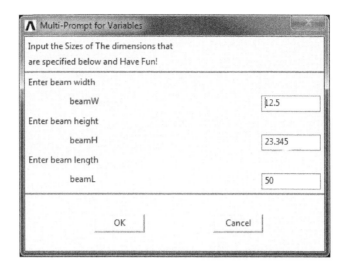

Figure 4.2: Example MULTIPRO Prompt

4.4 Workshop 3: Prompting the User

In this workshop we will take our simple bracket tool to the next level and replace the hardcoded parameter values with a MULTIPRO prompt.

1: Add MULTIPRO and *CSET commands *after* the parameter definitions to prompt the user for all geometric parameters in a single window. Use the parameter definitions to set default values.

```
MULTIPRO,'START',4
    *CSET,1,3,W,'ENTER WIDTH',W
    *CSET,4,6,H,'ENTER HEIGHT',H
    *CSET,7,9,D,'ENTER DEPTH',D
    *CSET,10,12,Rb,'ENTER BEND RADIUS',Rb
MULTIPRO,'END'
```

2: Add *ASK commands to prompt the user for the hole radius and bracket thickness. Use the parameter definitions to set default values. Enclose the parameter names in percent signs to substitute parameter values (covered later).

```
*ASK,Rh,radius of hole,%Rh%
*ASK,T,thickness of bracket,%T%
```

3: Save as bracket3.mac, open ANSYS using the jobname bracket3, and execute bracket3.mac. For the initial run, accept defaults when prompted for the hole radius and the bracket thickness.

4: Re-execute the bracekt3 macro using various values for the parameters specified through the user prompt. What happens when you make the hole diameter larger than the width or depth of the bracket? How can you prevent the user from making this mistake? (Hint: *IF/*ENDIF, covered later.)

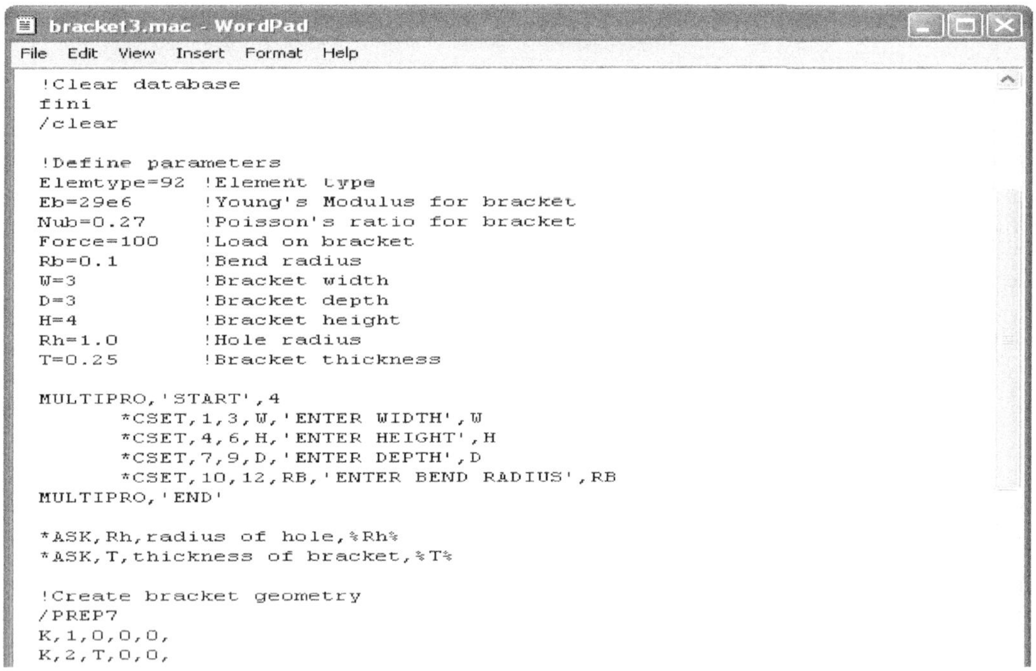

```
!Clear database
fini
/clear

!Define parameters
Elemtype=92 !Element type
Eb=29e6        !Young's Modulus for bracket
Nub=0.27       !Poisson's ratio for bracket
Force=100      !Load on bracket
Rb=0.1         !Bend radius
W=3            !Bracket width
D=3            !Bracket depth
H=4            !Bracket height
Rh=1.0         !Hole radius
T=0.25         !Bracket thickness

MULTIPRO,'START',4
      *CSET,1,3,W,'ENTER WIDTH',W
      *CSET,4,6,H,'ENTER HEIGHT',H
      *CSET,7,9,D,'ENTER DEPTH',D
      *CSET,10,12,RB,'ENTER BEND RADIUS',RB
MULTIPRO,'END'

*ASK,Rh,radius of hole,%Rh%
*ASK,T,thickness of bracket,%T%

!Create bracket geometry
/PREP7
K,1,0,0,0,
K,2,T,0,0,
```

Figure 4.3: Workshop 3 results after step 4

End of Workshop

4.5   Debugging Tips

A good practice to debug programs is to copy and paste a line or several lines of commands from the APDL file to the command input window to run the program line by line.

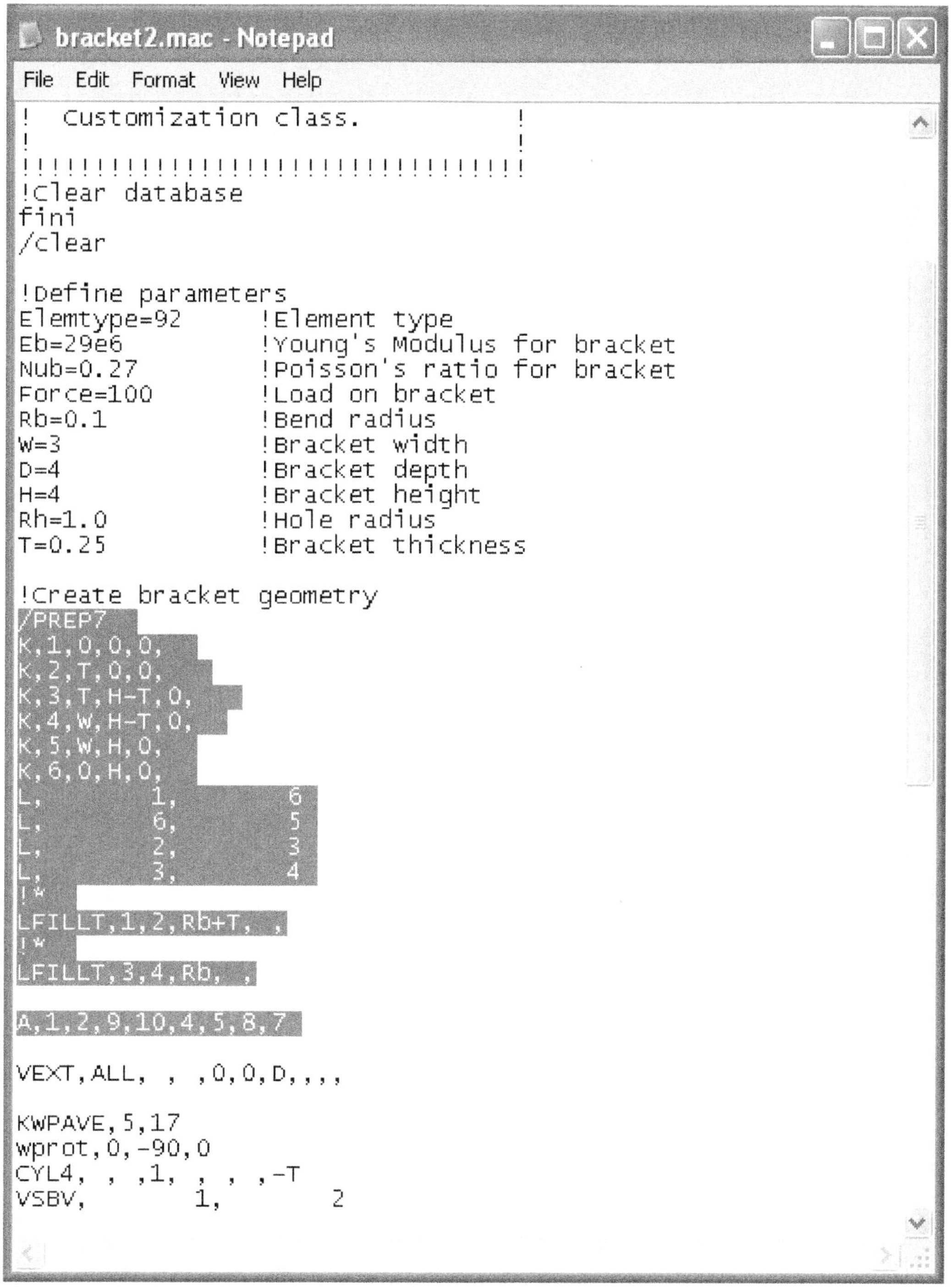

bracket2.mac - Notepad

File Edit Format View Help

```
!   Customization class.            !
!                                   !
!!!!!!!!!!!!!!!!!!!!!!!!!!!!!!!!!!!!!
!Clear database
fini
/clear

!Define parameters
Elemtype=92        !Element type
Eb=29e6            !Young's Modulus for bracket
Nub=0.27           !Poisson's ratio for bracket
Force=100          !Load on bracket
Rb=0.1             !Bend radius
W=3                !Bracket width
D=4                !Bracket depth
H=4                !Bracket height
Rh=1.0             !Hole radius
T=0.25             !Bracket thickness

!Create bracket geometry
/PREP7
K,1,0,0,0,
K,2,T,0,0,
K,3,T,H-T,0,
K,4,W,H-T,0,
K,5,W,H,0,
K,6,0,H,0,
L,         1,         6
L,         6,         5
L,         2,         3
L,         3,         4
!*
LFILLT,1,2,Rb+T, ,
!*
LFILLT,3,4,Rb, ,

A,1,2,9,10,4,5,8,7

VEXT,ALL, , ,0,0,D,,,,

KWPAVE,5,17
wprot,0,-90,0
CYL4, , ,1, , , ,-T
VSBV,       1,        2
```

Figure 4.4: Cutting and Pasting Lines of Code

The highlighted text is then copied into the command line shown in the figure below.

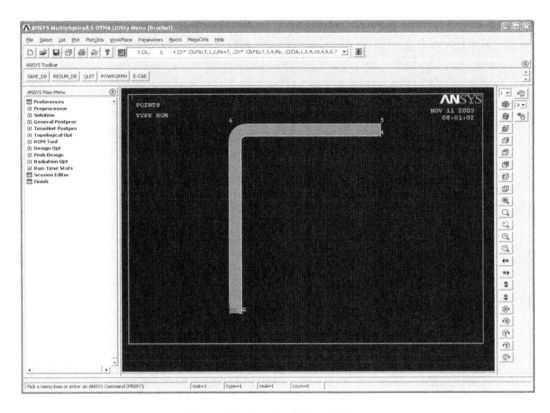

Figure 4.5: Result of Pasted Lines

Another method for debugging is to insert the /EOF command into the APDL file to end the program run at that point.

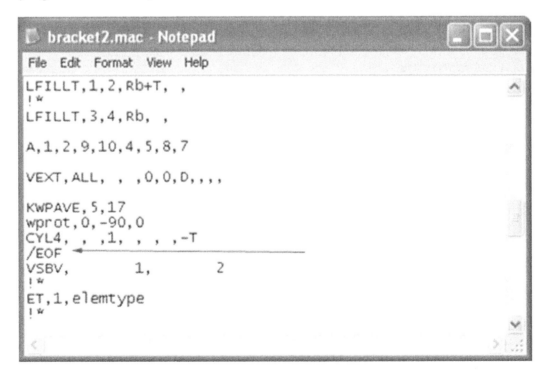

Figure 4.6: Inserting an EOF Command to Stop Execution

Using the debugging tips and following the steps to the workshop, your results should be as follows:

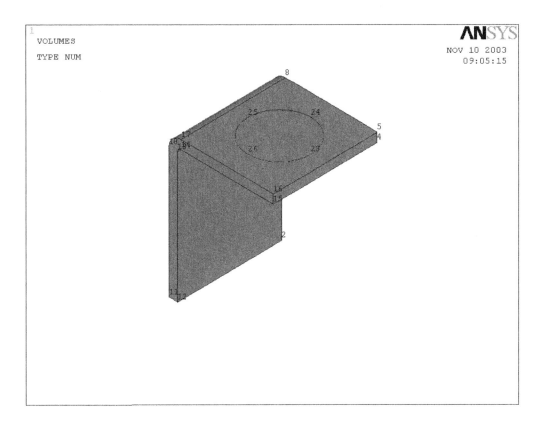

Figure 4.7

4.6   Status Bar

Another way to interface with the user is to use a Status Bar. Note: This is an undocumented command. The ANSYS program uses it and you can access it, but the commands are not documented. It is a very simple little dialog box with 23 little boxes that fill in from left to right:

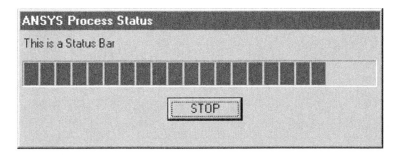

Figure 4.8: Process Status Bar

When the user presses stop, the value of _RETURN is set to 1. So to use it, you want to check _RETURN to see if the user has stopped, and if so, exit your loop. Also, if you try and update the status after the user has clicked Stop, then the status bar will no longer work properly.

A status bar can be displayed to show progress and allow the user to stop a program Loop. In fact, you can just show a stop button and not a graph. It should be used whenever a long *do-loop or similar operations take place.

A status bar can be created with *ABSET. This does not display the status bar, you need to us *ABCHECK to do that.

```
*ABSET,TITLE,ITEM
    ! TITLE: Text string up to 40 characters long
    ! ITEM: describes type of bar
    !       BAR: STATUS with no STOP button
    !       KILL: STOP button only
    !       BOTH: STATUS bar with STOP button
```

Once created, you display then update the status bar with the *ABCHECK command:

```
*ABCHECK,percent,newtitle
    ! Percent: A number from 0 to 100 that shows the percent completed
    ! Newtitle: A new string to display as the title. Use this to
    !           provide the user with additional feedback.
```

When your loop is completed, remove the status bar with *ABFINI

4.7   Displaying Messages

Another way to interface with the user is to display messages. In fact, this is the most common method and works in the GUI and in batch files.

You display messages to the user with *MSG command. What is unique about the *MSG command is that it uses two lines. The first is a standard comma delimited APDL command and the second is a format statement.

```
*MSG,Lab,VAL1,VAL2,VAL3. . .,VAL8
    ! Lab: controls style and termination as follows:
    !     INFO: Message with no heading and echoed to the
    !           Output window or file. Macro keeps running. (Default)
    !     NOTE: Message with "NOTE" heading and echoed to the
    !           Output window or file. Macro keeps running.
    !     WARN: Message with "WARNING" heading, and writes message
    !           to JOBNAME.ERR. Macro keeps running.
    !     ERROR: Message with "ERROR" heading, and writes message to
    !            JOBNAME.ERR. Macro keeps running.
    !     FATAL: Message with "FATAL ERROR" heading, writes message to
```

```
!         JOBNAME.ERR, and terminates the run
!      UI: Message with "NOTE" Heading and displayed in a GUI
!            message box (recommended for interactive use)
! VAL1 through VAL8 are values to be shown, including text strings.
```

The line immediately following the *MSG command line is required to be a format statement. The format statement consists of any text you want displayed with 'C' format statements imbedded. The 'C' format statements are called "enhanced descriptors"

Example:

```
*MSG,UI,23,1e-3
The Peak is (%I), and the Minimum is(%G)
```

Displays:

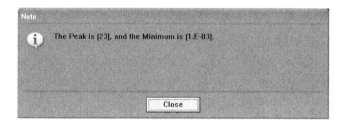

Enhanced descriptors come in very handy to create well formatted messages. They are standard 'C' descriptors:

```
%w.pE           w is field width
%w.pG           p is precision (number of significant digits)
%w.pF           p is number of decimal places
%%        a single percent sign
%wC; %wS   character string (can go up to 128 characters)
%-wC; %-wS       left justify string
%wX       w is number of blank characters
%wI       integer format preceded by w blank characters
%0wI           pad integer with loading zeros rather than blanks
%0w.pI         w is field width; p is number of characters filled
```

Pay special attention to the padding capabilities, they come in very handy.

4.8   Writing to a File and Showing It

When you need to share a large amount of data with a user, the best way to do that is use the *VWRITE command (covered later) to put the information in a formatted way to a text file. Then use *LIST,fname,ext to display the file if the user is running interactive. Or if batch, the user can look at the file using a text editor.

Chapter 5: Program Flow in APDL

5.1 Introduction

After gaining an understanding of parameters and their use, the next step to using APDL as a programming language is to understand how to control the flow of your macros with program flow controls. The "if's", "do's", and "call's" that almost all languages have.

These tools entered APDL slowly, starting with the ancient but useful *goto and progressing to some nice controls that are downright modern... well modern when compared with programming languages from the 1980's. The key to really getting power from APDL is to use these control statements efficiently to allow your programs to do more, and to be more general.

5.2 Calling Macros and Passing Arguments

The first way to control the flow of a program is to call a macro from within a macro, or from the command line. When you do that, you can pass up to 19 arguments (parameters) to a macro. These are local to the macro being executed, meaning that once the macro is executed, the arguments are deleted by the program. Arguments are assigned to variables named ARG1 through ARG9 and AR10 through AR19. AR20 through AR99 may be used within the macro itself (e.g. AR20=ARG1+ARG2) but cannot be passed to it via the command line.

Example (mymacro.mac):

```
/prep7
Block,,arg1,,arg2,,arg3
Sphere,arg4
VSBV,1,2
finish
```

To execute, type:

```
Mymacro,4,3,2.2,1
```

5.3 Nesting

Macros can call other macros, similar to a subroutine. Nesting allows calls up to 20 levels deep, similar to the F77 CALL function. Arguments can be passed when the macro is called, or you can define variables that are global and therefore available to the macro.

Example:

Macro MYSTART.MAC

```
/prep7
view,-1,-2,-3
mysphere,1.2
finish
```

Macro MYSPHERE.MAC

```
sphere,arg1
```

5.4   *GO and Labels

The original way to control program flow in APDL was the *GO. This is like the old GoTo in Basic. It works with labels and allows you to skip around in your macro:

```
*GO, Base
! BASE:  What to do when the line is executed
!            :label - Go to the first line in the program that starts
!                     with :label. It will wrap if necessary and start
!                     searching at the top of the file if needed
!                STOP: Causes an exit of the ANSYS program
```

Labels are simply a line in the macro that starts with a colon (:) that is followed by a unique 8 character string. They work with *GO and *IF commands.

It cannot be used in a *IF or *DO block.

The fact is that the *GO command really does not make much sense now that we have *IF and *do statements, but users find clever ways to use it. One such use is that instead of commenting out a large block of commands, simply put a *GO,:SKIP1 in front of the block and :SKIP1 at the end. This will avoid the tedious task of placing exclamation points in front of every line you want to skip.

5.5   *IF Branching

The *IF command is the most basic and most used flow control statement in APDL. Like most "If" statements in most languages, it has the form if something is true, do something. It also supports "else" and "else if" statements. Use it to make decisions on what code is executed and what is not.

The *IF command has the following format:

```
*IF,VAL1,OPER1,VAL2,BASE1,VAL3,OPER2,VAL4,Base2
! VAL1,OPER1,VAL2,BASE1:  A Boolean logic statement where VAL1
!                         is compared to VAL2 based on the
!                         VALUE of OPER1. If the result is TRUE, the
!                         operation in BASE1 is executed
```

```
! VAL3,OPER2,VAL4,BASE2:   A Boolean logic statement where VAL3
!                          is compared to VAL4 based on the
!                          VALUE of OPER2. The result is combined !
!                          with the result of VAL1,OPER1,VAL2 using the
!                          value of BASE1. If the resulting Boolean
!                          combination is true, BASE2 is executed.
! OPER1/OPER2:  These are the comparison operations that result in a
!               a TRUE or FALSE return:
!              EQ: True if VAL1/3 equals VAL2/4
!              NE: True if VAL1/3 does not equal VAL2/4
!              LT: True if VAL1/3 is less than VAL2/4
!              GT: True if VAL1/3 is greater than VAL2/4
!              LE: True if VAL1/3 is less than and equal to VAL2/4
!              GE: True if VAL1/3 is greater than and equal to VAL2/4
!            ABLT: True if absolute value of VAL1/3 is less than
!                  the absolute value of VAL2/4
!            ABGT: True if absolute value of VAL1/3 is less than
!                  the absolute value of VAL2/4
! BASE1/BASE2: Action to execute if Boolean is true
!          :label - A user defined lable beginning with a color (:),
!                  8 char maximum.  The command will skip to :label
!          STOP: This causes an exit from the ANSYS program if in batch
!                mode. If in interactive mode, the macro stops
!          EXIT: Exit the current do-loop
!          CYCLE: Skip to the end of the current do-loop, but
!                do not exit
!          THEN: Makes this an if-then-else statement and the lines
!                lines following are executed if the operation is TRUE
!                if it was FALSE, then it skips to the next *ENDIF,
!                ELSE, or *ELSEIF.
!   AND, OR, XOR: Valid for BASE1 only. How to combine the results of
!                VAL1,OPER1,VAL2 and VAL3,OPER2,VAL4
```

As you can see, this is a complicated command with a lot of options. You can combine two Boolean operations if you want by using the extra arguments: VAL3,OPER2,VAL4,BASE2. But this can make your code hard to follow, so it is recommended that you nest *IF statements instead.

Most of the time people use a BASE1 of THEN and combine it with a terminating statement of *ELSE, *ENDIF, and *ELSEIF. When BASE1 is THEN you must always have an *ENDIF at least and as many *ENDIF and *ELSEIF commands as you need to balance things out.

When a statement is evaluated as true and BASE1 is THEN, the APDL commands between that statement and whatever terminates the statement are executed, including calls to other macros. This figure shows it graphically:

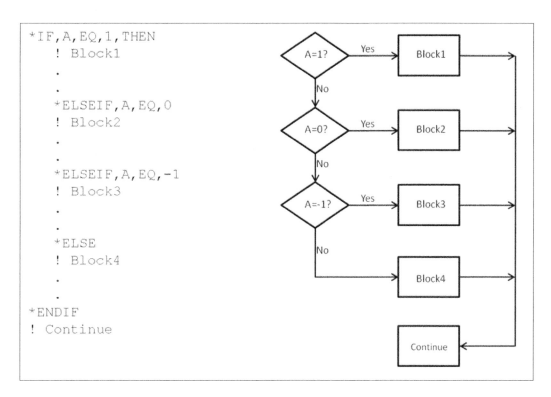

```
*IF,A,EQ,1,THEN
   ! Block1
   .
   .
   .
   *ELSEIF,A,EQ,0
   ! Block2
   .
   .
   .
   *ELSEIF,A,EQ,-1
   ! Block3
   .
   .
   .
   *ELSE
   ! Block4
   .
   .
   .
*ENDIF
! Continue
```

Figure 5.1: Examples of *IF branching

The terminators `*ELSE` and `*ENDIF` have no arguments. `*ELSEIF` has the following arguments:

```
*ELSEIF, VAL1, Oper1, VAL2, Conj, VAL3, Oper2, VAL4
```

These are just like the arguments for `*IF` except that there is no `BASE1` or `BASE2`. A `THEN` is implied. Most of the time you just use `VAL1,OPER1,VAL2` but if you wish to have two Boolean operations combined, use `CONJ` to specify `AND`, `OR`, or `XOR`.

You can nest `*IF` statements, and people often do go three or four levels deep. But beyond that, the code can get very confusing and it is usually better to redo the logic you are trying to represent.

The label `BASE` can also be very handy. One nice feature in it is that it goes to the first occurrence of: label it finds in the macro. If it does not find one by the end of the file, it starts at the beginning. This gives the programmer a way to "jump backwards" in a program. It is similar to the GOTO statements in older programming languages.

The `EXIT` and `CYCLE` options for `BASE` can be very powerful. They allow you to either exit a `*DO` loop or stay in the loop but go to the end of the loop, skipping any commands between the `*IF` and the `*ENDDO`. These can both be done with: LABEL but this approach is easier to follow.

It is recommended that you also use indentation when using `*IF` statements. The command interpreter does not care but it does make your macros more readable. Another suggestion for readability is if you have a very large block of code between an `*IF` and an `*ELSE`/`*ELSEIF`/`*ENDIF` it is a good idea to put that part of the macro in its own macro. That makes it easier to see where the program is in the `IF`/`ELSE` logic.

5.6   Checking Execution Status

Parameters `_STATUS` and `_RETURN` are generated each time ANSYS executes a command. This can be used with a `*IF` statement to give feedback to the user, or even stop execution of the macro.

`_STATUS` returns status of execution. The possible values are:

0	No Error
1	Generated a Note
2	Generated a Warning
3	Generated an Error

`_RETURN` stores the number of created solid model entities created in the last geometry creation command executed. See help for more information.

5.7   *REPEAT

Another old-school command is `*REPEAT`. It re-executes the command on the line preceding the `*REPEAT` command the specified number of times, incrementing the arguments in the fields by the values you specify.

```
*REPEAT,NTOT,VINC1,VINC2,VINC3,VINC4,VINC5,VINC6,VINC7,VINC8,VINC9, VINC10,
VINC11
```

`NTOT` is not the number or repeats to execute, but the total number of times to execute the command including the first time it is executed. So if you want to execute the command 4 more times, `NTOT = 5`.

Example:

```
E,1,2
*REPEAT,5,0,1
```

It executes 4 more times (5 total), incrementing argument 2 by 1 each time. It is the same as:

```
E,1,2
E,1,3
E,1,4
```

```
E,1,5
E,1,6
```

5.8 *DO Loops

*DO Loops allow you to loop through a series of commands a specified number of times.
*DO and *ENDDO mark beginning and end of loop.

```
*DO, Par, IVAL, FVAL, INC
! Par: The counting parameter to use.
! IVAL: The initial value for Par. It can be a real number and there
!        is no default.
! FVAL: The final or highest value allowed for Par. Once Par is greater
!        than FVAL, the program jumps to the command after *ENDDO
! INC: The value to add to Par at the start of each loop.  Defaults to
!        1 but can be any integer or real number, and can be negative.
```

The *ENDDO command has no arguments. You can nest *DO loops up to 20 levels deep.

The program simply executes the commands between the *DO and *ENDDO until:

- Par is greater than FVAL
- An *IF statement evaluates to true with a CYCLE or EXIT operation on it
- A *CYCLE or *EXIT command is encountered.

When the command interpreter gets to the *ENDDO, it increments Par by Inc then jumps back up to the *DO command where Par is compared to FVAL. If it is still less than or equal to FVAL, it executes the block again.

*CYCLE and *if,val1,oper,val2,cycle (when true) work the same way. They cause the command interpreter to jump to the matching *ENDDO, increment by Inc, and go back to the *DO command.

*EXIT and *if,val1,oper,val2,exit (when true) also work the same way. But they cause the command interpreter to immediately exit the do loop and execute the command right after the corresponding *ENDDO. Par is not incremented.

For example:

```
*DO,I,1,5         ! For I = 1 to 5:
  LSREAD,I          ! Read load step file
  OUTPR,ALL,NONE   ! Change output controls
  ERESX,NO
  LSWRITE,I          ! Rewrite load step file
*ENDDO
```

As with the *IF statements, it is a good idea to use indentation and to place large blocks of code into macros that are called.

You can modify the value of Par in the loop, but it is not recommended because it is not standard and can cause confusion.

5.9   Implied Do Loops

The problem with *DO loops is that they can be very slow. The commands in the loop are executed by the command interpreter and can take some time to parse and execute. They are more efficient because they take up fewer lines of the macro and run much faster. When the command interpreter sees an implied do-loop, it actually executes the command in a special FORTRAN routine in one call, rather than a call for each execution.

The down side is that they only work with a single command. If you need to execute multiple commands, they need to be in a *DO loop or each command must be an implied do loop.

To use an implied do loop, substitute (*start:end:increment*) for the appropriate argument in a given command (note placement of colons and parentheses), where *start* is the starting value, *end* is the ending value, and *increment* is the increment (defaults to 1).

For example, to create a series of keypoints from x = 0 to x = 10 spaced 2 units apart, execute the following:

```
k,,(0:10:2),0,0
```

The *DO loop would be:

```
*do,i,0,10,2
    k,,i,0,0
*enddo
```

Implied do loops come in very handy when working with arrays. The indices of the arrays can be incremented in the implied format rather than a *DO loop, really speeding things up.

5.10   Comparison Operators

Comparison operators are a shortcut for deciding which of two numbers to use in an expression. If you have two parameters, and you want to use either the larger or the smaller in an expression, you can use a comparison operator.

Place the two numbers in parentheses with a greater (>) or lesser (<) than sign between them instead of a single parameter.

Example

```
*if,a,lt,b,then
    xyz = a*Y**2
*else
    xyz = b*y**2
 *endif
```

Can be replaced by:

```
xyz=(a<b)+y**2
```

5.11 *RETURN

Sometimes you just want to leave a macro. The various options with *IF allow you to exit a *DO loop or even the ANSYS program, but not just the macro.

```
*RETURN, Level
! Level: The level of macro calls to go to. A negative value will jump
!        "up" by the number given.  A positive value will jump to the
!        level number given.
```

*RETURN is usually used with an *IF statement to detect user error and check the ability of the remainder of the macro to be executed, and if needed, safely exit the macro. Its use can also avoid multiple levels of if-then-else statements that can get very confusing and hard to track.

The concepts of levels can be very confusing and it is not recommended that a program try and skip levels. The default is to exit the current macro file, and that is the recommended use.

5.12 Workshop 4: Using *IF and *MSG

In this workshop, we would like to provide the user with the option of creating the hole and to specify the hole diameter through arguments via the command:

```
bracket4,hole,Rh
```

Where `hole` = `1` if a hole is desired, `0` if not and `Rh` = `radius` of the hole.

If an argument is left blank, it will default to zero, causing errors in the macro execution if a hole is desired. We will have to specify a default hole diameter to prevent these errors from occurring.

Also, in Workshop 3, we added prompts to allow the user to input the bracket dimensions. One potential problem is that it is possible for the hole to be too large for the bracket, removing too much material from the top. We would like to alter the macro to prevent this error.

First, review the beginning of Workshop 3 macro:

```
fini
/clear
Elemtype=92
Eb=29e6
Nub=0.27
Force=100
Rb=0.1
W=3
D=3
H=4
!Prompt for hole radius and thickness
*ASK,Rh,radius of hole,1
*ASK,T,thickness of bracket,0.25
/PREP7
K,1,0,0,0,
K,2,T,0,0,
K,3,T,H-T,0,
K,4,W,H-T,0,
K,5,W,H,0,
K,6,0,H,0,
!etc...
```

Now we need to modify the macro to accept arguments, define defaults, and do error checking with user feedback.

1: Copy the file bracket3.mac to bracket4.mac. Open bracket4.mac using a text editor.

2: Delete the line: *ASK,Rh,radius of hole,1

3: To resolve the first problem, we should create a default value for the hole radius: arg2. We will use the same value as in prior workshops: Rh=1. It would also be a good idea, and not too difficult, to prevent the user from entering a negative value for the hole radius. Also, in order to facilitate macro editing, we should set Rh equal to arg2.

Add the following lines before the parameter definitions in the bracket4.mac file:

```
*IF,arg2,LE,0,THEN
     arg2=1
*ENDIF
Rh=arg2
```

4: The diameter of the hole, if present, cannot exceed the minimum dimension on the top area. There should also probably be a certain amount of material between the hole and the edge for structural integrity. Using *IF/*ENDIF, *MSG, and *RETURN alert the user if the hole is too large. Use the undocumented function MIN(Val1,Val2, etc.), which returns the minimum value among the arguments. Lastly, if the user receives this error, the macro should be terminated.

The following should be inserted after the line `*ASK,T,thickness of bracket,%T%`

```
    mindim=MIN(W-T-Rb,D)                !Set parameter mindim
    mindim = 0.9*mindim             ! allow for 10% edge material
   *IF,2*Rh,GE,mindim,THEN
         *MSG,ERROR,2*Rh,mindim
The hole diameter of %G exceeds the minimum bracket platform%/& dimension of
%G.  Run aborted.
         mindim=          !Erases parameter mindim
         *RETURN
    *ENDIF
```

5: Add conditional (*IF/*ENDIF) statements around the hole creation commands to create the hole if arg1 = 1.

Place the *IF/*ENDIF around the commands that create the cylinder and do the Boolean subtract;

```
*IF,arg1,EQ,1,THEN
    KWPAVE,5,17
    WPROT,0,-90,0
    CYL4, , ,Rh, , , ,-T
    VSBV, 1, 2
*ENDIF
```

6: Since there may or may not be a hole in the bracket, the area number definition will vary. Because of this, it is a good idea to select the loaded and constrained areas by location and apply the appropriate boundary conditions. Also, area numbers generated from the extrusion operation may change in later versions of ANSYS. First we will modify the code to fix the bottom area, finding the area by location.

Delete the following FLST/FITEM/P51X commands

```
         FLST,2,1,5,ORDE,1
         FITEM,2,3
         !*
         /GO
         DA,P51X,ALL,
```

and replace with

```
         ASEL,S,LOC,Y,0       !Select bottom area by location (y=0)
         DA,ALL,ALL
         ALLSEL
```

7: Next we need to grab the area where the X equals the Width value

Delete the command to select area 7

```
ASEL,S, , ,7
```

and replace with

```
ASEL,S,LOC,X,W        !Select right area by location (x=W)
```

8: Save the file as bracket4.mac.

9: Now exercise the macro:

Start ANSYS using the jobname bracket4 and execute the bracket4 macro with hole creation by typing "bracket4,1,0.9" in the Input window.

Try typing "bracket4" in the Input window with no local parameters specified.

Verify that the macro works with or without hole creation, with an oversized hole radius, etc.

END OF WORKSHOP

5.13   Workshop 5: Do Loops

In this workshop, we will modify the bracket macro (cleaned up for your convenience) to create a number of holes along the center of the top platform specified by arg1, each with radius specified by arg2. We will also ramp the load over a series of load steps dictated by arg3. The number of holes will default to 1, the hole radius will default to 0.1, and the number of load steps will default to 1. In Workshop 5A we will create the holes using *DO/*ENDDO. In Workshop 5B we will use an implied do loop.

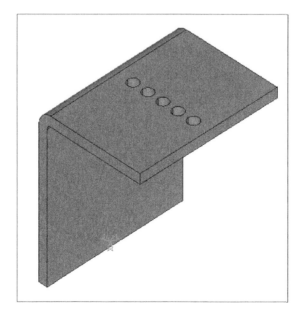

Figure 5.2: Multiple Hole Bracket

1: Copy the file bracket5.mac (located in the inputs folder with the course material) to bracket5a.mac and open with a text editor.

2: Add the following statements before the parameter definitions, but after the FINI and /CLEAR lines to set argument defaults:

```
*IF,arg1,LE,0,THEN
     arg1=1                 !Default to 1 hole
*ENDIF
*IF,arg2,LE,0,THEN
     arg2=.1                      !Default hole radius = 0.1
*ENDIF
*IF,arg3,LE,0,THEN
     arg3=1                 !Default to one loadstep
*ENDIF
```

3: Set the Rh parameter to be equal to arg2

```
Rh=arg2              !Hole radius
```

4: Offset the workplane to the location of the first hole using the WPOFFS command. This should be inserted after the WPROT command.

```
wprot,0,-90,0
wpoffs,(W-T-Rb)/(arg1+1)-(W-T-Rb)/2
```

5: Using a *DO/*ENDDO loop create the holes as shown below. The CYL4 command will be modified and *DO and *ENDDO statements added before and after it. (Suggestion: Enter /EOF after the VSBV command and debug at this point)

```
*DO,i,1,arg1
     CYL4,(i-1)*((W-T-Rb)/(arg1+1)), ,Rh, , , ,-T
*ENDDO
VSBV, 1, ALL
```

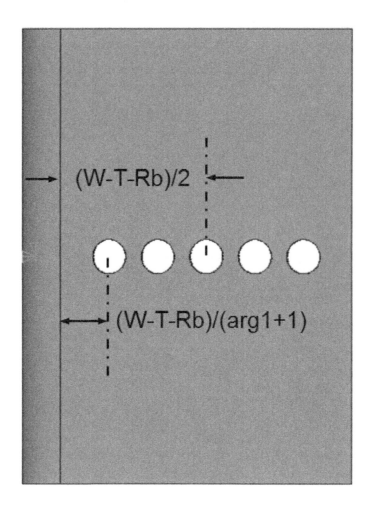

Figure 5.3: Geometry for Hole Spacing

6: Using a *DO/*ENDDO loop, ramp the load starting from the initial value for parameter FORCE over a series of loadsteps. The load for each loadstep will be equal to FORCE multiplied by the loadstep number. The *DO loop will be inserted after the bottom face is constrained and all entities are selected.

```
*DO,j,1,arg3
        ASEL,S,LOC,X,W
        NSLA,S,1
        *GET,NUMNODE,NODE,,COUNT, , , ,
        F,ALL,FY,-Force*j/NUMNODE
        ALLSEL,ALL
        LSWRITE,j
*ENDDO
```

7: Save the macro as bracket5a.mac

8: Enter ANSYS and type in bracket5a,3,.125,5. Debug your macro if needed and try different values. See what happens if the number of holes or size of holes is too large.

9: To make it more robust, add *IF statements and *MSG commands to alert the user if the number of holes and loadsteps specified are not integers (Hint: NINT(arg1)-arg1 should be zero). Also add checks to verify that the holes are not subtracting too much volume from the bracket.

10: If you are really feeling motivated, modify the macro to query the user for the load direction and/or magnitude for each loadstep. Example:

```
*DO,j,1,arg3
    ASEL,S,LOC,X,W
    NSLA,S,1
    *GET,NUMNODE,NODE,,COUNT, , , ,
     DIR=            !Necessary to clear DIR parameter between load steps
    *ASK,DIR,direction of loading (X, Y, or Z),'Y'
    *ASK,FORCE,force magnitude,100
    !Apply load in x, y, or z direction based on user input
    *IF,DIR,EQ,'X',THEN
          F,ALL,FX,FORCE/NUMNODE
    *ELSEIF,DIR,EQ,'Y',THEN
          F,ALL,FY,-FORCE/NUMNODE
    *ELSEIF,DIR,EQ,'Z',THEN
          F,ALL,FZ,-FORCE/NUMNODE
    *ELSE
    !Notify user and stop macro if X, Y, or Z is not input for DIR
          *MSG,ERROR,
          Must specify X, Y, or Z for load direction!  Macro terminated
          *RETURN
    *ENDIF
*ENDDO
```

11: Modify bracket5a.mac to use an implied do loop to create the holes instead of *DO/*ENDDO and save file as bracket5b.mac.

First, review the existing do-loop:

```
*DO,i,1,arg1
      CYL4,(i-1)*((W-T-Rb)/(arg1+1)), ,Rh, , , ,-T
*ENDDO
```

Then delete the *DO and *ENDDO

Notice how the value of i is in the equation, not just an integer value. So we cannot just replace I with (1:arg1,1). We need substitute the equation at i=1 and i=arg1:

```
i=1:  0
i=arg1:  (arg1-1)*((W-T-Rb)/(arg1+1))
```

Then we need to figure out what the increment is. And that is not so hard when you realize the increment is simply the distance between the holes:

increment: (W-T-Rb)/(arg1+1)

Then place each one in the (start:end:inc) format:

```
CYL4,(0:(arg1-1)*((W-T-Rb)/(arg1+1)):(W-T-Rb)/(arg1+1)),,Rh,,,,-T
```

Although not the easiest to read, this is a very concise way to define it and it executes very quickly. Using implied do loops can make an order of magnitude difference in the speed at which your macro executes.

12: Test and debug. Try different values.

END OF WORKSHOP

Chapter 6: Information Retrieval in ANSYS

6.1 Introduction

In previous chapters we have covered the features found in most programming languages. Now we will move on to something that makes APDL special, and delivers the power that makes APDL so much more than a way to automate a command file: how to retrieve information from your ANSYS database.

The ANSYS Mechanical APDL program stores a large and detailed database in memory that contains almost every bit of information about your model. By using the information retrieval capabilities in APDL, your macros can get at that information, do calculations with it, and make decisions based upon what you find. This capability and its ease of use is really what sets APDL apart from most languages used for customizing engineering software.

6.2 Retrieving Information

You can query ANSYS for most information including the model, settings, and results. *GET retrieves information from the database, such as a keypoint location or first principal stress at a node, and stores it in a scalar parameter.

Whereas *GET is a standard comma delimited command, the "Get functions" and "inquiry functions" are shorthand notations for getting information out of the database that can be used to define parameters or in-line with other commands.

6.3 *GET

*GET is a very powerful command that every user should get to know. Although it does not access every type of information found in the database, it accesses a large portion of it. The syntax and usage is the same for getting nodal locations or the name of the job. It returns a single value, or scalar value. You use *VGET to access multiple values.

The key to understanding *GET is that you access information by a hierarchy. There is no *GET,,X_VALUE_OF_NODE,32. Instead you first give it the entity type you are looking for (NODE), the type of value you are looking for (LOC for location), then if needed, more specific information about the type of value (X). You usually have to also specify an entity number.

The *GET command looks like:

```
*GET,Par,Entity,ENTNUM,Item1,IT1NUM,Item2,IT2NUM
! Par: the name of the parameter that you want the results placed in
! Entity: A keyword that describes the entity type you will be getting
!         information on
```

```
! ENTNUM: The number of the entity you want information on.  For some
!          entity types it is left blank
!          Item1:  The name of the item you want to get for the
!                  entity type
!          IT1NUM: The number, or more often the label, that further
!                  specifies the information you want
!    Item2,IT2NUM: A second set of qualifiers that are sometimes used
```

*GET Documentation

There are several hundred documented, and a handful of undocumented *GET combinations. The Documented commands can be found by looking up the *GET command in the Command Reference. The following is a screen capture of the Entity=NODE portion of the manual page. As you can see, each Entity type describes what to use for ENTNUM, ITEM1, and IT1NUM. It also describes the information obtained in detail.

Table: *GET Preprocessing Items, Entity = NODE

colspan		

Entity = NODE, *ENTNUM* = *N* (node number)

*GET, *Par*, NODE, *N*, Item1, IT1NUM, Item2, IT2NUM

Item1	IT1NUM	Description
LOC	X, Y, Z	X, Y, Z location in the active coordinate system. Alternative get functions: NX(*N*), NY(*N*), NZ(*N*). Inverse get function. NODE(x,y,z) returns the number of the selected node nearest the x,y,z location (in the active coordinate system, lowest number for coincident nodes).
ANG	XY, YZ, ZX	THXY, THYZ, THZX rotation angle.
NSEL		Select status of node *N*. -1=unselected, 0=undefined, 1=selected. Alternative get function: NSEL(*N*).
NXTH		Next higher node number above *N* in selected set (or zero if none found). Alternative get function: NDNEXT(*N*).
NXTL		Next lower node number below *N* in selected set (or zero if none found).
F	FX, MX, ...	Applied force at selected node *N* in direction *IT1NUM* (returns 0.0 if no force is defined, if node is unselected, or if the DOF is inactive). If *ITEM2* is IMAG, return the imaginary part.
D	UX, ROTX, ...	Applied constraint force at selected node *N* in direction *IT1NUM* (returns a large number, such as 2e100, if no constraint is specified, if the node is unselected, or if the DOF is inactive). If *ITEM2* is IMAG, return the imaginary part.
HGEN		Heat generation on selected node *N* (returns 0.0 if node is unselected, or if the DOF is inactive).
NTEMP		Temperature on selected node N (returns 0.0 if node is unselected)
CPS	Lab	Couple set number with direction Lab = any active DOF, which contains the node *N*.

Entity = NODE, *ENTNUM* = 0 (or blank)

*GET, *Par*, NODE, 0, Item1, IT1NUM, Item2, IT2NUM

Item1	IT1NUM	Description
NUM	MAX, MIN	Highest or lowest node number in the selected set.
NUM	MAXD, MIND	Highest or lowest node number defined.
COUNT		Number of nodes in the selected set.
MXLOC	X, Y, Z	Maximum X, Y, or Z node coordinate in the selected set (in the active coordinate system).
MNLOC	X, Y, Z	Minimum X, Y, or Z node coordinate in the selected set (in the active coordinate system).

Note: If ANSYS creates internal nodes during solution, the internal nodes will not be included. You can include them by using *KINTERNAL*, a seventh *GET command argument specific to *Entity* = NODE. The command syntax is:

*GET, *Par*, NODE, 0, Item1, IT1NUM, Item2, IT2NUM, KINTERNAL

The options for the *KINTERNAL* key are *(blank)*, - count only external nodes, and *INTERNAL*, - count all nodes, including internal nodes.

Figure 6.1: Typical *GET Help Page Table

Some examples for using *GET include:

```
*GET,BCD,ELEM,97,ATTR,MAT      ! BCD = Material number of element 97
*GET,V37,ELEM,37,VOLU          ! V37 = volume of element 37
*GET,EL52,ELEM,52,HGEN         ! EL52 = value of heat generation in element 52
*GET,OPER,ELEM,102,HCOE,2      ! OPER = heat coefficient of element 102,face2
*GET,TMP,ELEM,16,TBULK,3       ! TMP = bulk temperature of element 16,face3
*GET,NMAX,NODE,,NUM,MAX        ! NMAX = maximum active node number
*GET,HNOD,NODE,12,HGEN         ! HNOD = value of heat generation at node 12
*GET,COORD,ACTIVE,,CSYS        ! COORD = active coordinate system number
```

It would be a good idea to go to the ANSYS Mechanical APDL Command Reference and scan through the tables in the *GET command just to get a feel for the breadth and width of commands available. As you can see in the help page, they are sorted first by what modules in the program the information exists in:

- General Items
- Preprocessing Items
- Solution Items
- Postprocessing Items
- Probabilistic Design Items

Then each section is broken down by entity type. The best way to find what you are looking for is to skip to the module you are interested in, and then use the "Find in Page" function of the help system to find what you are looking for.

Undocumented *GET Commands

Over the years developers have added a wealth of undocumented *GET commands at the request of users, or for use internally. You should never use them in a macro that you think might last for a while, because they commands may break or even go away in future releases. But if you are brave and are willing to take the risk, some of them are very handy. Many have been documented through the years so there are not as many as there used to be:

Two of the more useful undocumented *GET commands are:

```
*get,parm,ACTIVE,,SYNAME,,START,1  ! the name of the current
                                   ! operating system e.g. windows, or
                                   ! linux
*get,parm,ACTIVE,,update  ! the update version number of the release of
                          ! ANSYS MAPDL you are using
```

The website www.ansys.net is a great resource for undocumented commands, as well as macros, tips and tricks, etc.

The *GET,Par,COMMON Command

The most common undocumented *GET command is *GET,par,COMMON. The vast majority of scalar values in ANSYS Mechanical APDL are stored internally as FORTRAN COMMON block values. So, if a user really wants to get at that information they can use *GET,par,COMMON to specify which common block the data is in, what type of value it is (INT/REAL) and then where it is in the common block.

Here are some examples:

```
*GET,Par,COMMON,,STEPCM,,INT,30
!   Retrieves number of nodal diameters
*GET,Par,COMMON,,CFPRP7,,REAL,13; *GET,Par,COMMON,,CFPRP7,,INT,63
```

```
!   Retrieve global element edge length and number of divisions,
!   respectively
*GET,Par,NODE,n,NTEMP
!   Retrieves applied structural temperatures
```

The command looks like this:

```
*GET,Par,COMMON,,filename,,int_or_real,varnum
! filename: The name of the common block file (*.inc),
! int_or_real: Designates whether the parameter is int (integer) or
!              real (double precision)
! varnum: The variable number.
```

*cm.inc files are located in the installation directory under ansys/custom/include. This subdirectory is available only after performing a custom installation, although *GET,Par,COMMON,… will work regardless.

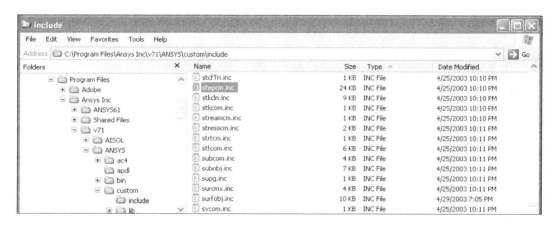

Figure 6.2: Example of Include Directory

For example, to retrieve the current element size setting file CFPRP7.inc can be referenced. We want the element size which is in elsize. Yes, sometimes you just have to guess by the name. Then we start counting numbers in the common block. When we find an array, the size of the array is the number of number. So adigit(4,3) counts as 12 numbers.

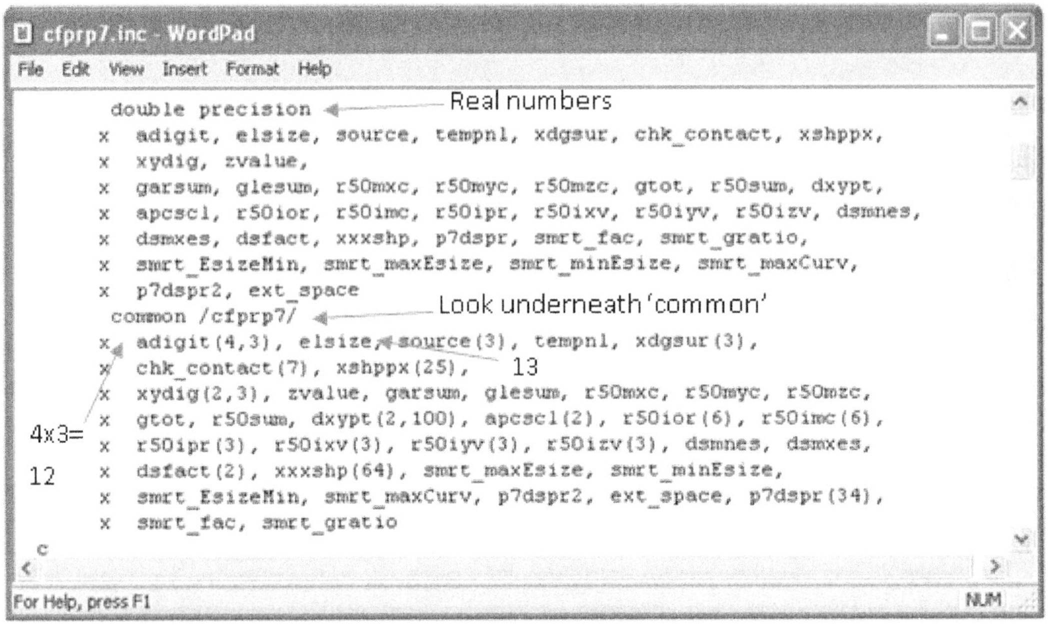

Figure 6.3: Example Common Block Information

So to get that information, you would use:

```
GET,Par,COMMON,,CFPRP7,,REAL,13
```

6.4   GET Functions

Shorthand notations, called "get functions" exist for frequently used *GETs. They allow multiple *GETs on one line and eliminate the necessity for parameter creation. They can be found in the GET function summary under APDL Programmer's Guide in the Help System. It should be noted that the *GET documentation mentions alternate get functions, when applicable.

For example:

```
*GET,L1,NODE,1,LOC,X
*GET,L2,NODE,2,LOC,X
MID = (L1+L2)/2
```

Can be simplified to:

```
MID=(NX(1)+NX(2))/2
```

More examples of get functions are as follows:

```
KSEL(k)
 ! returns select status of keypoint k (1=selected, 0=undefined,
 ! -1=unselected)
```

```
NY(n)
  ! returns y-location of node n
LZ(L, lfrac)
  ! returns z-coordinate of line at length fraction lfrac
KP(X, Y,  Z)
  ! returns keypoint nearest location X, Y, Z
DISND(n1, n2)
  ! returns distance between nodes n1 and n2
KNEAR(k)
  ! returns keypoint nearest keypoint (k)
AREAND(n1, n2, n3)
  ! returns area of triangle with vertices at n1, n2, and n3
UX(n)
  ! returns resulting x-displacement at node n
TEMP(n)
  ! returns resulting temperature at node n
```

6.5   /INQUIRE

Another useful tool for getting information from the database is /INQUIRE. It is sort of like the *GET commands but it fills a string array rather than a parameter. It is usually the best way to find out information about the current job, files, and environment variables.

```
/INQUIRE,StrArray,Func,Val1,Val2,Val3
! StrArray: The name of an array to place the results in. You do
!            not have to predefine the array
! Func: A label that defines what you are looking for
! Val1,Val2,Val3: Varies depending on what Func is
```

The following are values for Func that retrieve system and file information. They require no additional values for Val1-Val3:

- LOGIN returns path of login (UNIX) or default (Windows) directory
- DOCU returns path of ANSYS docu directory
- APDL returns path of ANSYS apdl directory (undocumented)
- PROG returns path of ANSYS executable directory
- AUTH returns path of directory in which license file resides
- USER returns name of user currently logged in
- DIRECTORY returns pathname of current (working) directory
- JOBNAME returns jobname up to 250 characters
- RSTDIR Returns rst directory from a FILE command
- RSTFILE Returns rst file name from a FILE command
- RSTEXT Returns rst file extension from a FILE command
- PSEARCH Returns path used for "unknown command" macro (/PSEARCH command).

- OUTPUT Returns the current output file name (/OUTPUT command).

Another use for the /INQUIRE command is obtaining the value of system level environment variables. To do so you use

```
/INQUIRE,StrArray,ENV,Envname,Substring
```

Envname refers to the environment variables name and is not case sensitive. Substring is a number used to parse an environment variable list and return the nth value in a colon or semicolon separated list. If Substring is 0, then the whole list is returned.

As an example:

```
/inquire,pth,ENV,path
! Returns: C:\Program Files\ANSYS Inc\v140\Framework\bin\Win64;C:\Prog
!ram Files (x86)\AMD APP\bin\x86_64;C:\Program Files (x86)\AMD APP\bin

/inquire,pth,env,path,1
! Returns: C:\Program Files\ANSYS Inc\v140\Framework\bin\Win64

/inquire,pth,env,path,2
! Returns: C:\Program Files (x86)\AMD APP\bin\x86_64
```

You can find information about the current title values for plotting with:

```
/INQUIRE,strarray,Title,Title_num
```

Where Title_Num is the title number. If Title_num is blank, 0, or 1 then the string specified with /TITLE is returned. If it is between 2 and 5 it refers to the subtitles defined with /STITLE.

The final variation on /INQUIRE is used to get information on a specific file:

```
/INQUIRE,Par,Func,Fname,Ext
```

For this variation the returned value is a number except when DATE is specified for Func. The values for Func and what they return are:

- EXIST returns 1 if the file exists, 0 if not
- DATE returns date stamp on file
- SIZE returns file size in Mb
- WRITE returns 1 for write permission, 0 if no
- READ returns 1 for read permission, 0 if no
- EXEC returns 1 for execute permission, 0 if no
- LINE returns number of lines in an ASCII file

6.6   Inquiry Functions

Inquiry functions are similar to get functions, but undocumented, and also provide shortcuts to database item retrieval. They take the form of XXinqr(entrid,key) or XXXiqr(entid,key). Their most common use involves a number of defined or selected entities, sets, or attributes like this:

- XXinqr(0,12) returns number of defined entities/sets/attributes
- XXinqr(0,13) returns number of selected entities/sets/attributes
- XXinqr(0,14) returns highest numbered entity/set/attribute
- Examples:
    - ndinqr(0,12) returns number of defined nodes
    - elmiqr(0,13) returns number of selected elements
    - csyiqr(0,14) returns highest coordinate system number
    - arinqr(ar,-3) returns real constant for area ar
    - etyiqr(et,1) returns select status for element type number et
    - kpinqr(k,-4) returns node number attached to keypoint k (if meshed)
    - erinqr(4) returns number of warning messages issued
    - lsinqr(L,-8) returns number of element divisions in existing mesh for line L
    - ndinqr(n,-5) returns solid model attachment for node n
    - vlinqr(v,-6) returns number of elements in volume v

For a much more extensive listing, see Appendix A, taken from the ANSYS Solutions article on inquiry functions, written by John Crawford.

6.7   Workshop 6: Retrieving Data

In this workshop we will modify bracket2.mac to use *GET commands, get functions, and inquiry functions where applicable.

1: Copy bracket2.mac to bracket6.mac. Open bracket6.mac

2: Modify the L and A commands to use appropriate get functions to create lines and areas through existing keypoints based on their locations, rather than their numbers. The A command should be all one line.

```
L,KP(0,0,0),KP(0,H,0)
L,KP(0,H,0),KP(W,H,0)
L,KP(T,0,0),KP(T,H-T,0)
L,KP(T,H-T,0),KP(W,H-T,0)

A,KP(0,0,0),KP(T,0,0),KP(T,H-T-RB,0),KP(T+RB,H-T,0),KP(W,H-
T,0),KP(W,H,0),KP(RB+T,H,0),KP(0,H-RB-T,0)
```

3: Modify the KWPAVE command to incorporate get functions as follows:

```
KWPAVE,  KP(Rb+T,H,0),KP(W,H,D)
```

4: Delete the *GET,NUMNODE,... line after NSLA,S,1 since it will no longer be needed after the next step.

5: Replace NUMNODE in the F command with the inquiry function ndinqr(0,13) since this will return the number of selected nodes.

```
F,ALL,FY,-Force/ndinqr(0,13)
```

6: Next we would like to retrieve the maximum downward displacement and the node at which it occurs and display this information to the user.

7: First, enter the command SOLVE before FINISH.

8: After FINISH, enter the following:

```
/POST1                        !Enter the general postprocessor
NSORT,U,Y                        !Sort all y-displacements in the model
*GET,uymax,SORT,0,MIN            !Retrieve minimum (max. absolute)
                                 !value from sort
*GET,n_uymax,SORT,0,IMIN    !Retrieve node number at which
                     !minimum sort value occurs
```

9: Display displacement information to the user in a message box using the *MSG command. Enter the following after the last *GET line:

```
*MSG,UI,uymax,n_uymax
Maximum downward deflection = %G at node %I
```

10: Save file. Run and debug if necessary.

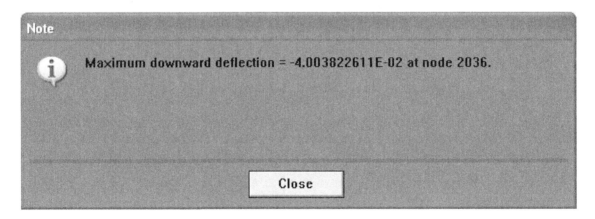

Figure 6.4: Message from Macro

End of Workshop

Chapter 7: Arrays, Tables, and Strings

7.1 Introduction

Because ANSYS Mechanical APDL is a Finite Element Program, it has lots of vector and matrix information in it. Loads over time, nodal coordinates, stress tensors, non-linear material properties, etc... In order to deal with this type of data, as well as with character data, APDL has Array, Table, and String parameters.

In this chapter we will go over the fundamentals of arrays, tables, and strings as well as introduce the commands and functions that can be used to fill them, do math with them, and modify the database with them.

7.2 Arrays

In ANSYS 7.1 and earlier, the array options were One, Two, or Three Dimensional arrays (row, column, plane). In 8.0 and later, 4-D and 5-D (books and shelves) arrays and tables are also possible. There are four types of arrays:

- ARRAY
    - o Just like F77 arrays of real numbers
    - o Indices are sequential starting from 1
- CHAR
    - o Character array
    - o Each element consists of up to eight characters
    - o Indices are sequential starting from 1
- TABLE
    - o Special array used for linear interpolation
    - o Indices begin at 0
- STRING
    - o Used to store long character strings, limit of 128 characters
    - o Column and plane indices begin at 0

Arrays can contain up to 2^{31}-1 bytes of data. For double precision, this translates to (2^{31}-1)/8 data items since each data item is 8 bites.

A typical 1D array, which is actually a vector, is m rows long and one column wide. Rows are identified by row number I, 1 to m and can be accessed as name(i).

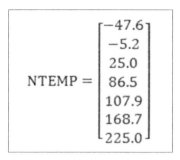

Figure 7.1: Sample 1D Array

A 2D array is m rows long by n columns wide. Rows are identified by row number I, 1 to m while columns are identified by column number j, 1 to n and can be accessed as name(i,j)

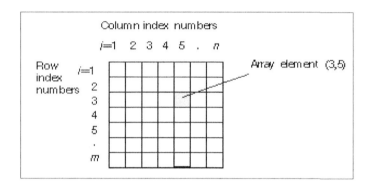

Figure 7.2: Sample 2D Array

A 3D array is the same as 2D, but with planes added. It is n rows, by m columns by p planes where planes are identified by plane number k, 1 to p. A 3D array element can be accessed as name(i,j,k).

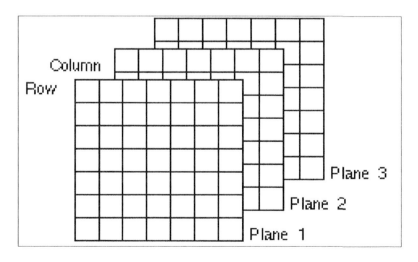

Figure 7.3: Sample 3D Array

Before you fill an array, you should use the *DIM command to define the array dimensions. This is not always true for 1D arrays, as some commands automatically dimension arrays when they are filled. But in general it is a good idea to predefine your arrays with a *DIM.

```
*DIM,Par,Type,IMAX,JMAX,KMAX,Var1,Var2,Var3,CSYSID
! Type: The type of multidimensional parameter being defined
!    ARRAY: A 1, 2, or 3D array
!     ARR4: Same as ARRAY, but defines a 4D array
!     ARR5: Same as ARRAY, but defines a 5D array
!     CHAR: Character array
!    TABLE: A special 1, 2, or 3D array with 0th row and columns
!           have non-integer indices, allow for automatic interpolation
!     TAB4: Same as TABLE, but defines a 4D array
!     TAB5: Same as TABLE, but defines a 5D array
!   STRING: String array
! IMAX: Number of rows. Defaults to 1
! JMAX: Number of columns. Defaults to 1
! KMAX: Number of planes.  Defaults to 1
! Var1: For a table, the variable name for the rows.
!        Default is Row
! Var2: For a table, the variable name for the columns.
!        Default is Column
! Var3: For a table, the variable name for the planes.
!        Default is Plane
! CYSID: A coordinate system ID to associate with the array
```

For example:

```
*DIM,AA,,4               !Type ARRAY is default, dimension 4[x1x1]
*DIM,XYZ,ARRAY,12        !Type ARRAY array, dimension 12[x1x1]
*DIM,FORCE,TABLE,5,3,2   !Type TABLE array, dimension 5x3x2
*DIM,T2,,4,3             !Dimensions are 4x3[x1]
*DIM,CPARR1,CHAR,5       !Type CHAR array, dimension 5[x1x1]
```

7.3   Specifying Array Values

To specify an array value, use the *SET or "=." An array can be defined one column at a time, up to ten rows. For Example:

```
XYZ(1)=59.5,42.494,-9.01,-8.98,-8.98,9.01,-30.6,51
XYZ(9)=-51.9,14.88,10.8,-10.8
```

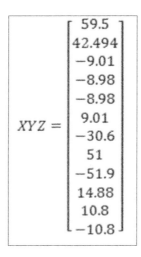

$$XYZ = \begin{bmatrix} 59.5 \\ 42.494 \\ -9.01 \\ -8.98 \\ -8.98 \\ 9.01 \\ -30.6 \\ 51 \\ -51.9 \\ 14.88 \\ 10.8 \\ -10.8 \end{bmatrix}$$

Figure 7.4: Example Array

Notice that the starting location of the array element is indicated by the row index number of the parameter (1 in the first command, 9 in the second command).

For character arrays, enclose the text in single quotes:

```
*dim,ldnames,char,9
ldnames(1) = 'startup','taxi_out','takeoff','climb'
ldnames(5) = 'cruise','approach','land','taxi_in','soak'
```

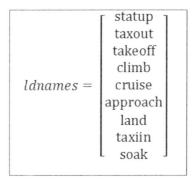

$$ldnames = \begin{bmatrix} statup \\ taxout \\ takeoff \\ climb \\ cruise \\ approach \\ land \\ taxiin \\ soak \end{bmatrix}$$

Figure 7.5: Example Character Array

Here's another example:

```
T2(1,1)=.6,2,-1.8,4          ! defines (1,1),(2,1),(3,1),(4,1)
T2(1,2)=7,5,9.1,62.5         ! defines (1,2),(2,2),(3,2),(4,2)
T2(1,3)=2E-4,-3.5,22,.01     ! defines (1,3),(2,3),(3,3),(4,3)
```

Which results in:

$$T2 = \begin{bmatrix} 0.6 & 7.0 & 0.0002 \\ 2.0 & 5.0 & -3.5 \\ -1.8 & 9.1 & 22.0 \\ 4.0 & 62.5 & 0.01 \end{bmatrix}$$

Figure 7.6: Example 2D Array

A table example would be this:

```
FORCE(1)=0,560,560,238.5,0
FORCE(1,0)=1E-6,.8,7.2,8.5,9.3
```

$$FORCE = \begin{matrix} 1E-6 \\ 0.8 \\ 7.2 \\ 8.5 \\ 9.3 \end{matrix} \begin{bmatrix} 0.0 \\ 560.0 \\ 560.0 \\ 238.5 \\ 0.0 \end{bmatrix}$$

Figure 7.7: Example Table Array

The first "=" command defines the five array elements of the TABLE array FORCE. The second "=" command define the index numbers in the j = 0 column. An alternative to defining 0 row or column values is the *TAXIS command.

7.4 Editing Arrays in the GUI

To edit or fill arrays using the GUI, use *VEDIT. The menu options are:

Utility Menu > Parameters > Array Parameters > Define/Edit

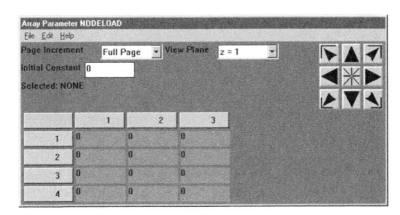

Figure 7.8: Array in the GUI

With tables, the concept of the row and column '0' index can be a bit difficult to get your head around. We have found that creating or at least displaying the table, or at least part of it, in the GUI can be very helpful to drive home the concept:

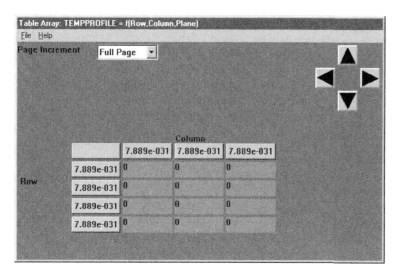

Figure 7.9: Table in the GUI

7.5   *VGET

When the *GET command was covered it was noted that it works to retrieve scalar values. But because so much of what is stored in the database exists as a collection of multiple points, a tool is needed to retrieve that information.

To retrieve multiple values into an array, use the *VGET command. The *VGET command loops on a specified field to "*GET" over a range. To use the *VGET command, the array must already be defined with *DIM. Examples of the *VGET command are as follows:

```
*VGET, node_loc(1,1), NODE, 1, LOC, X
! Fills array named node_loc with the X-location of nodes starting
!  with node 1 to the end of the array


*VGET, prin_str(1,1), NODE, 50,S,1
! Fills prin_str array with the 1st principal stresses starting
!  with node 50 through the size of the array


*VGET,elem_dat(1,1), ELEM, 7, LOC, X,,,4
! Fills array named elem_dat with the node number positions
!  for all nodes in ELEM 7
```

The *VGET command is much more limited than the *GET command and occasionally, arrays need to be filled by using *GET in a *DO loop or an implied do-loop.

7.6   VGET (Without the asterisk)

VGET (without they asterisk) retrieves a TimeHistory Postprocessor (POST26) variable and stores it in an array. It is good for exporting Time History data to an Excel spreadsheet. The format for VGET is this:

```
VGET,ParR,varnum,tstart,kcplx
!   ParR is the array parameter to store data to.  Must be
!     defined with *DIM.
!   varnum is the variable number to store.
!   tstart is the time or frequency value at which to begin to retrieve
!     varnum values (rounds off to closest time or frequency).
!     Defaults to first item.
!   kcplx = 0 to retrieve real part of varnum,
!           1 to retrieve imaginary part (e.g. harmonic load analysis
!           Defaults to 0.
```

7.7   /INQUIRE

The /INQUIRE command with the format of /INQUIRE,strarray,Func retrieves text system information and stores to the string parameter strarray. strarray does not have to be defined using *DIM. If it does not exist, it will be created automatically. The Func component has many options which include the following:

- LOGIN returns path of login (UNIX) or default (Windows) directory
- DOCU returns path of ANSYS docu directory
- APDL returns path of ANSYS apdl directory (undocumented)
- PROG returns path of ANSYS executable directory
- AUTH returns path of directory in which license file resides
- USER returns name of user currently logged in
- DIRECTORY returns pathname of current (working) directory
- JOBNAME returns jobname up to 250 characters
- ENV returns value(s) of an environment variable
- TITLE returns title or subtitle(s)

/INQUIRE with the call: /INQUIRE,Par,Func,file,ext can return information about a specific file. The Func call has the following options:

- EXIST returns 1 if the file exists, 0 if not
- DATE returns date stamp on file
- SIZE returns file size in Mb
- WRITE returns 1 for write permission, 0 if no
- READ returns 1 for read permission, 0 if no
- EXECUTE returns 1 for execute permission, 0 if no
- LINE returns number of lines in an ASCII file

7.8 Using String Arrays in Commands

One of the more useful things that you can do with string arrays is use them in commands instead of a variable or a value. Concatenation takes place during execution so you can get very clever with this.

To use a string array in a command, simply enclose the array name and starting index in percent signs. For example:

```
/INQUIRE,job,JOBNAME
/INQUIRE,workdir,DIRECTORY
/TITLE,File %job(1)% located in %workdir(1)%
```

Figure 7.10: Title Created with String Array Substitution

To display a string array, issue *STAT,strarray. For example, *STAT.workdir will return:

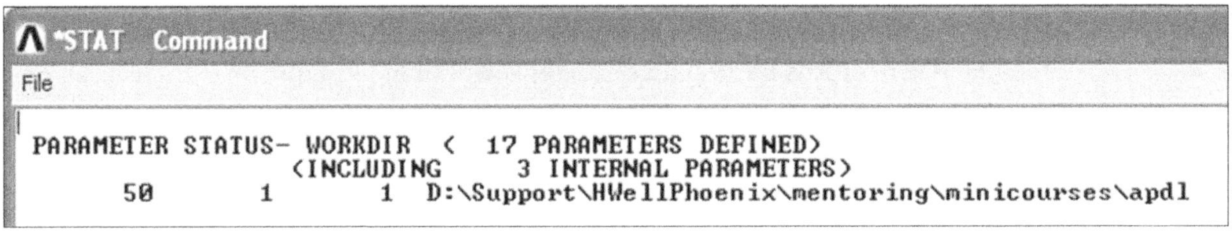

Figure 7.11: Listing Contents of a String Array with *STAT

A common use of string substitution is to use a character array to specify parameter or array names in commands. The following examples stores the X, Y, and Z location of the nodes in the model into three arrays: NDX, NDY, and NDZ. But instead of having three *VGET commands, we loop over an array DD that contains the characters X, Y, and Z.

```
*get,nnd,node,,count
*dim,dd,char,3
dd(1) = 'x','y','z'
*do,j,1,3
    *dim,nd%dd(j)%,,nnd
    *do,i,1,nnd
        *vget,nd%dd(j)%,node,i,loc,%dd(j)%
    *enddo
*enddo
```

A more complex example is using this capability to loop through a series of runs and post process them:

```
nmrns = 5          !Number of runs
*do,i,1,nmrns
    finish
    /filname,PN123_Run%i%    !Change jobname
    /post1
    set
    /show,pn123_rst_run%i%  !Set name for plot files
    do_post !Macro to do post processing
    /show,close    !close plotfile
    /show,term     !return output to screen
*enddo
```

7.9   Converting String Arrays to Character Parameters

To convert a string array to a character parameter, simply issue: char=strarray(1). The character parameters will be truncated to 32 characters. To store more of the string array to character parameters, issue: char2=strarray(33), char3=strarray(65), etc. For example:

```
wdpart1=workdir(1)
wdpart2=workdir(33)
```

which results in the values shown in following figure:

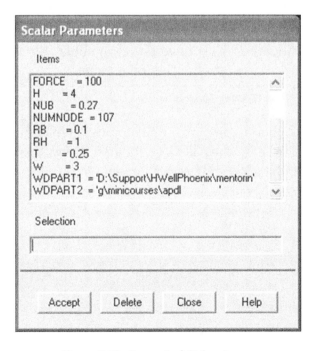

Figure 7.12: Converted String Arrays

7.10 String Functions

APLD provides a large number of string functions that are similar to those found in most programming languages. This really opens up what a user can do and can be very powerful.

They work like any other parameter function, except that they work on strings.

The first set of functions are used to convert strings to numbers, including octal and hex numbers.

Function	Description
VALCHR(string)	Converts a string that contains a valid decimal or integer number as text into a double precision parameter
VALOCT(string)	Converts a string that contains a valid Octal number as text into a double precision parameter
VALHEX(string)	Converts a string that contains a valid Hexadecimal number as text into a double precision parameter
CHRVAL(num)	Converts a decimal number into a text string
CHROCT(num)	Converts a number into a text string octal number
CHRHEX(num)	Converts a number into a text string hexahedral number

They are self-explanatory and easy to use.

The next set of functions are common in most programming language, although the syntax may be a little different. They allow you to find strings in strings, justify, truncate, remove spaces, and all that good stuff you often need to do with strings:

Function	Description
STRSUB(Str1,nLoc,nChar)	Returns a substring of the characters in Str1. Returns characters number nLoc to nLoc+nChar as a string.
STRCAT(Str1,Str2)	Concatenates Str2 onto the end of Str1. Returns a string.
STRFILL(Str1,Str2,nLoc)	Fill in Str1 with Str2 starting at character number nLoc in Str1. Returns a string.
STRCOMP(Str1)	Compress Str1 by removing all the spaces in Str1. Returns a string.
STRLEFT(Str1)	Left justify Str1 by removing all leading spaces from Str1. Returns a string.
STRPOS(Str1,Str2)	Returns the position in Str1 where Str2 can be found. If it is not found, it returns 0. Returns a number.
STRLENG(Str1)	Returns the length of Str1, excluding training spaces. Returns a number.
UPCASE(Str1)	Converts all the characters in Str1 to Upper Case. Returns a string.
LWCASE(Str1)	Converts all the characters in Str1 to Lower Case. Returns a string.

Again these functions are simple and easy to use. The key is to make sure that you use their names correctly and do not try and get too fancy.

7.11 Filling Arrays

To automatically fill arrays, use *VFILL with the format:

```
*VFILL, ParR, Func, CON1, CON2,. . ., CON10
! Func:
!   DATA = specify values
!   RAMP = ramp from CON1 by incrementing by CON2
!   RAND = Random numbers between CON1 and CON2 (defaults to 0,1)
!   GDIS = Random numbers in a Gaussian distribution where CON1
!          is the mean and CON2 is one standard deviation
```

```
!            (defaults to 0,1)
!    TRIA = Random numbers based on triangular distribution where
!           CON1 is the lower bound, CON2 is the location of the peak,
!           CON3  is the upper bound
!    BETA = Random numbers based on beta distribution. See help.
!    GAMM = Random numbers based on gamma distribution. See help.
```

To fill arrays from a file use *VREAD. For example:

mydata.txt contains:

```
1.5      7.8  12.3
15.6  -45.6  42.5
```

Read it with:

```
*DIM,EXAMPLE,,3,2
*VREAD,EXAMPLE(1,1),mydata,txt,,2
(3F6.1)
```

*VREAD is covered in more detail in the section reading and writing from and to files.

7.12   Vector Operations

Once you have information in arrays, there are many useful things you can do with them using vector operations. We divide these into two groups: Calculations and Operations Filters

Calculation Operations on vectors can be done using the following list of vector functions:

    *VOPER Performs operations
    *VFUN   Performs a function that produces a new array
    *VSCFUN Performs a function that produces a scalar value
    *VITRP   Interpolates a table for each array member

*VOPER performs an operation between two arrays (*Par1* and *Par2*) and stores the results in a third array parameter (*ParR*). The format for *VOPER is as follows:

```
*VOPER,ParR,Par1,Oper,Par2,Con1,Con2
```

The options for *Oper* are:

    Math operations: ADD, SUB, MULT, DIV
    Comparison operations: MIN, MAX, LT, LE, EQ, NE, GE, GT
    Calculus operations: DER1, DER2, INT1, INT2
    Vector operations: DOT, CROSS
    Indexing: GATH, SCAT

*VFUN performs an operation on a single array (*Par1*) and stores the results in a second array parameter (*ParR*). The call for *VFUN is:

```
*VFUN,ParR,Func,Par1,Con1,Con2,Con3
```

The options for *Func* are:

> Math Functions: NINT, PWR, SQRT
> Trig functions: SIN, COS, TAN, ASIN, ACOS, ATAN, SINH, COSH, TANH
> Log Functions: LOG, LOG10, EXP
> Data management: ASORT, DSORT, COMP, EXPA
> Principle stresses: DIRCOS, EULER
> Coordinate functions: TANG, NORM, LOCAL, GLOBAL

*VSCFUN determines scalar properties of an array parameter (*Par1*) and stores the results in a scalar parameter (*ParR*). You use it to find things like maximum and minimum values, or to find statistical information about an array like the sum, average, or standard deviation.

It has the call format of:

```
*VSCFUN,ParR,Func,Par1
```

Where *Func* can be:

> – MAX, MIN, LMAX, LMIN (MAX and MIN locations), FIRST (non-zero location), LAST (non-zero location), SUM, MEDI, MEAN, VARI, STDV, RMS, NUM (number of summed values)

*VITRP forms an array parameter (*ParR*) by the interpolation of a table (*ParT*) at row, column, and plane index designated by arrays *ParI*, *ParJ*, and *ParK*, respectively. The call format is:

```
*VITRP,ParR,ParT,ParI,ParJ,ParK
```

Filter Operations are carried out using the following commands. You need to execute each filter before a calculation vector command or any APDL command that uses an array is executed. Any filter values specified with these commands are erased once they are applied.

> *VCUM   Specifies if functions are cumulative or not
> *VABS   Makes following functions use absolute values
> *VFACT Applies a scale factor to following functions
> *VLEN   Sets length for vector functions
> *VMASK Specifies a mask array for functions

*VCUM indicates whether array parameter results should overwrite or be added to the existing results parameter. The call format is:

```
*VCUM,Key
```

where,

> Key = 0 overwrites results
> Key = 1 adds current results to new results. ParR = ParR (calculated in subsequent *Vxxx or *Mxxx operation) + ParR (existing)

*VABS takes the absolute values of the array parameters in the subsequent vector or matrix operation. The call format is:

```
*VABS,KABSR,KABS1,KABS2,KABS3
```

where,

> KABSR = 1 to take absolute value of results parameter (ParR),
>   0 = no change
> KABS1 = 1 to take absolute value of first parameter in operation (Par1),
>   0 = no change
> KABS2 = 1 to take absolute value of second parameter in operation (Par2),
>   0 = no change
> KABS3 = 1 to take absolute value of third parameter in operation (Par3),
>   0 = no change

*VLEN specifies the number of rows to which the subsequent vector operation should apply. By default, all rows are filled starting from a given index number. The call format is:

```
*VLEN,NROW,NINC
```

where,

> NROW = number of rows to be filled in the subsequent *Vxxx or *Mxxx operation
> NINC – perform the operation on every NINCth row

Example:

```
*DIM,LIST,,8
*VLEN,5,2
*VFILL,LIST(1),RAMP,1,1
```

This returns:

$$LIST = \begin{Bmatrix} 1 \\ 0 \\ 3 \\ 0 \\ 5 \\ 0 \\ 0 \\ 0 \end{Bmatrix}$$

*VMASK, Par specifies that array parameter *Par* should be used as the masking parameter in the subsequent vector operation. The masking parameter is generally filled with 1s, -1s, and 0s indicating the select status of an entity. This enables the subsequent *Vxxx or *Mxxx command to operate only on the selected entities. Frequently allows for a fast alternative to *Do/*ENDDO.

*VMASK is one of the more important vector tools because it works with vector operations that involve math, writing to files, or implied *DO Loops.

In this example, a force that is equal to the X position of each node is applied to that node. If there are gaps in node number, this skips over those gaps:

```
*get,mxnd,node,,num,max
*dim,nsl,,mxnd
*vget,nsl(1),node,1,nsel
*vmask,nsl(1)
f,(1:mxnd:1),FX,nx(1:mxnd:1)
```

7.13   Array Operations vs *DO Loops

As you become more and more familiar with APDL, look for opportunities to use array operations to perform the same types of functions as those performed by *DO loops. This can save you significant CPU time. The efficiency of vector operations over *DO loops can be shown with the following example:

1:   Type the following macro in and save as: fastnodearray.mac

```
*dim,nodesel,,ndinqr(0,14)
*dim,nodenums,,ndinqr(0,14)
*dim,fastnodes,,ndinqr(0,13)

*vget,nodesel(1),node,1,nsel
*vfill,nodenums(1),ramp,1,1
*vmask,nodesel(1)
*vfun,fastnodes(1),comp,nodenums(1)
```

2:   Type this macro in and save as: slownodearray.mac

```
*get,maxnode,node,0,num,max
*get,nnodes,node,0,count

*dim,slownodes,,nnodes

j=1
*do,i,1,maxnode
  *if,nsel(i),eq,1,then
    slownodes(j)=i
    j=j+1
  *endif
*enddo
```

3: Bring up one of the bracket models in isometric view and select a subset of nodes. List the nodes and note some of the numbers.

4: Execute the macro fastnodearray.mac. Note how long it takes to execute. List the FASTNODES array. Verify the selected node numbers.

5: Execute the macro slownodearray.mac. Note that it takes significantly longer to execute. List the SLOWNODES array and note that it contains the selected node numbers.

7.14 Table Arrays

A type TABLE array parameter consists of numbers (alphanumeric values are not valid) arranged in a tabular fashion. ANSYS can calculate, through linear interpolation, any values that fall in-between the explicitly declared array element values. A table array contains a 0 row and 0 column used for data-access index values, and unlike standard arrays, these index values can be real numbers. The only restriction is that the index values must be numerically increasing. A plane index value resides in the 0,0 location for each plane.

ANSYS linearly interpolates between entries. Instead of giving row or column integer, you give the value(s) you want to interpolate for. For example:

Given the following table:

$$A = \begin{array}{c} \\ 1.0 \\ 2.0 \\ 3.0 \end{array} \begin{array}{c} 1.0 \\ \left[\begin{array}{c} 12.0 \\ 28.0 \\ 146.4 \end{array}\right] \end{array}$$

Figure 7.13: Table Array

You would define it with:

```
a(1)=1,12,28,146.4
a(1,0) = 1,2,3
```

A(1.5) evaluates to 20.0 (halfway between 12.0 and 28.0)
A(1.75) evaluates to 24.0
A(1.9) evaluates to 26.4

An alternative to specifying a 0 row, column, or plane starting point for the index values is to use the *TAXIS command, discussed below.

7.15 Table Arrays for Boundary Conditions

A table may be used to define boundary conditions as a function of time, geometry, or temperature, by defining primary variables for the rows, columns, and planes.

Allowable primary variables include TIME, FREQ, X, Y, Z, TEMP, VELOCITY, PRESSURE and SECTOR.

You specify what primary variables refer to your row, column, or plane by specifying them in VAR1, VAR2, and VAR3 in the *DIM command.

X, Y, and Z can be in a user-specified coordinate system. To apply the table as a boundary condition, substitute the table name, enclosed in percent signs, for the load amount in a given command. The following example defines a table with temperatures that vary in X, Y, Z in coordinate system 11:

```
*dim,temptab,table,3,3,3,X,Y,Z,11
*taxis,temptab(1,1,1),1,0,5,10
*taxis,temptab(1,1,1),2,0,5,10
*taxis,temptab(1,1,1),3,0,5,10
temptab(1,1,1) = 10,100,10
temptab(1,2,1) = 12,150,10
temptab(1,3,1) = 10,90,7
temptab(1,1,2) = 12,120,12
temptab(1,2,2) = 15,180,15
temptab(1,3,2) = 17,90,12
temptab(1,1,3) = 20,200,20
temptab(1,2,3) = 22,250,20
temptab(1,3,3) = 20,290,27
BF,ALL,TEMP,%TEMPTAB%.
```

This applies a temperature to all selected nodes, based on the X,Y,Z location of each node.

Tables can also be used to define some real constant properties. SHELL181 can have varying thickness as a function of geometry. CONTA171-174 can have pressure or temperature dependent thermal contact conductance.

To see if a given load or boundary condition supports tables, look up the command for applying that load in help.

7.16 Nested Tables

In addition to primary variables like X, Y, Z, tables can also be made a function of independent parameters. This is accomplished via a "nested table," where values in one table are scaled based on values given in another parameter.

For example, consider a convection coefficient (HF) that varies as a function of rotational speed (RPM) and temperature (TEMP). The primary variable in this case is TEMP. The independent parameter is RPM, which varies with time. In this scenario, you need two tables: one relating RPM to TIME, and another table relating HF to RPM and TEMP.

```
*DIM,SYCNV,TABLE,3,3,,RPM,TEMP
SYCNV(1,0)=0.0,20.0,40.0
SYCNV(0,1)=0.0,10.0,20.0,40.0
SYCNV(0,2)=0.5,15.0,30.0,60.0
SYCNV(0,3)=1.0,20.0,40.0,80.0
*DIM,RPM,TABLE,4,1,1,TIME
RPM(1,0)=0.0,10.0,40.0,60.0
RPM(1,1)=0.0,5.0,20.0,30.0
SF,ALL,CONV,%SYCNV%
```

Nested tables can also be used to scale a table of, for example, pressure coefficients to a given maximum pressure value.

```
!Create nested table of pressure coefficients ( =< 1 in this case) as a
!function of X and Z locations
*DIM,CPTAB,TABLE,4,3,,X,Z
CPTAB(1,0)=0,1,2,3
CPTAB(0,1)=0,.5,.7,.9,.2
CPTAB(0,2)=2,.35,.6,.95,.3
CPTAB(0,3)=4,..25,.5,1,.46

!Create table to "scale" table of pressure coefficients
PMAX=80                       !Maximum pressure
*DIM,PSCALE,TABLE,2,,,CPTAB    !Row label is CPTAB, the table of Cps
PSCALE(1,0)=0,1          !Define 0th column
PSCALE(1,1)=0,PMAX            !Define first column
SF,ALL,PRESS,%PSCALE%  !Apply pressures by referring to PSCALE,
                       ! which calls CPTAB
```

7.17 4 and 5 Dimension Arrays and Table

Most users will simply use a one, two, or even three dimension array or table (row, column, plane). However, both arrays and tables support two more dimensions: books and shelves. Because this capability is a later addition to the program, it behaves a little differently. You need to add values for the size of the book (KMAX) and the shelf (MMAX) as well as variable names for each: VAR4 and VAR5

The first difference is in the `*DIM` command. For normal arrays and tables you use:

```
*DIM, Par, ARRAY, IMAX, JMAX, KMAX, Var1, Var2, Var3, CSYSID
*DIM, Par, TABLE, IMAX, JMAX, KMAX, Var1, Var2, Var3, CSYSID
```

For 4 dimension arrays or tables you use:

```
*DIM,Par,ARR4,IMAX,JMAX,KMAX,LMAX,Var1,Var2,Var3,Var4,CSYSID
*DIM,Par,TAB4,IMAX,JMAX,KMAX,LMAX,Var1,Var2,Var3,Var4,CSYSID
```

For 5 dimension arrays or tables you use:

```
*DIM,Par,ARR5,IMAX,JMAX,KMAX,LMAX,MMAX,Var1,Var2,Var3,Var4,Var5,CSYSID
*DIM,Par,TAB5,IMAX,JMAX,KMAX,LMAX,MMAX,Var1,Var2,Var3,Var4,Var5,CSYSID
```

It is important to be aware of this because if you look at the manual entry for *DIM it only lists the 3 dimension version of the command, and these variations are covered in the notes.

Once the array or table is defined you have to fill it using APDL commands, this size is not supported in the user interface. The same commands are used, but instead of supplying one, two or three indices values, you supply four or five.

The following is an example of defining a table in terms of location (X,Y,Z), Time, and Temperature. This is the most common usage of a five dimension table:

```
*dim,ldval,tab5,3,3,3,3,3,X,Y,Z,TIME,TEMP    ! table
*taxis,ldval(1,1,1,1,1),1,-2.3,0,3.4         ! X Range
*taxis,ldval(1,1,1,1,1),2,-1.2,0,1.8         ! Y Range
*taxis,ldval(1,1,1,1,1),3,-3.6,0,4.5         ! Z Range
*taxis,ldval(1,1,1,1,1),4,0,5,10             ! Time Range
*taxis,ldval(1,1,1,1,1),5,32,320,500         ! Temp Range

*do,ii,1,3
  *do,jj,1,3
    *do,kk,1,3
      *do,ll,1,3
        *do,mm,1,3
```

```
        !silly made up equation to fill the table with
        ldval(ii,jj,kk,ll,mm) = ii*.123+jj/.2+ll*kk+mm*JJ*JJ
    *enddo
  *enddo
 *enddo
 *enddo
*enddo
```

7.18   Table and Matrix Operations

Just like simple arrays that look like vectors, arrays that are tables or matrices have their own operators. These are very powerful and their use avoids the need to write complex programs or macros to handle large amounts of data.

Operations on tables functions:

> *TOPER   Performs operations on tables
> *TAXIS   Defines table index values

These commands allow you to operate on an entire plane, rather than just a single column.

*TOPER performs an operation between two tables (*Par1* and *Par2*) and stores the results in a third table (*ParR*). Although originally designed to do more operations, it only supports adding two tables right now. The call format is:

```
*TOPER,ParR,Par1,Oper,Par2,Fact1,Fact2,Con1
```

Where,

> Fact1 and Fact2 are scale factors applied to Par1 and Par2 respectively. Con1 is added to the result.
> Oper: ADD is the only available operation at this time

The command executes the equation (for all i,j,k): ParR(i,j,k) = FACT1*Par1(i,j,k) + FACT2*Par2(i,j,k) +CON1

If PAR2 is blank, then you can use the command to add a constant value (CON1) or scale PAR1 by FACT1.

PAR1 and PAR2 must have the same I, J, and K indices and be the exact same size.

A good example is scaling a unit pressure table by some value. If pressures are in PTAB() and you want to scale them by Pmax, use:

```
*TOPER,PTAB(1,1),PTAB(1,1),ADD,PTAB(1,1),Pmax,0,0
```

*TAXIS facilitates the definition of primary variable values when creating tables. It is an alternative to trying to define 0 row and 0 column indices and keeping all of that straight. Instead you specify the table, the axis you are defining, then the values.

The call format is,

```
*TAXIS,ParmLoc,nAxis,Val1,…,Val10
```

Where,

> ParmLoc is the starting index for table heading definition
> nAxis = 1 for row, 2 for column, 3 for plane, 4 for book, and 5 for shelf
> Val1 through Val10 are the table axis values
>> nAxis = All and Val1 = List will list the axis values to the output window.

For example, to define a table of temperature vs. X and Y locations per the table shown:

Table 7.1: Sample Pressure Table

		Y				
		0	1.2	2.4	3.1	4
	0	600	480	390	300	240
X	1.8	540	420	360	240	210
	2.5	450	360	270	210	150
	3	300	210	180	120	60

Use the following commands

```
*DIM,TEMPTAB,TABLE,4,5,,X,Y
*TAXIS,TEMPTAB(1,1),1,0,1.8,2.5,3
*TAXIS,TEMPTAB(1,1),2,0,1.2,2.4,3.1,4
TEMPTAB(1,1)=600,540,450,300
TEMPTAB(1,2)=480,420,360,210
TEMPTAB(1,3)=390,360,270,180
TEMPTAB(1,4)=300,240,210,120
TEMPTAB(1,5)=240,210,150,60
*TAXIS,TEMPTAB,all,list
```

Produces

```
LIST SCALES FOR ALL AXES
AXIS= 1  VALUES= 0.78886E-30  1.8000     2.5000     3.0000
AXIS= 2  VALUES=  0.0000      1.2000     2.4000     3.1000     4.0000
AXIS= 3  VALUES= 0.78886E-30
```

As you recall, a matrix is a parameter array with 2, 3, 4, or 5 dimensions. So they require their won commands to do operations or calculations with them. There are also some specialty functions available that save a lot of time and effort:

The operation commands for a matrix array are:

*MFUN	Copies or transposes a matrix
*MFOURI	Calculates coefficients for, or evaluates a Fourier series

*MFUN transposes or copies a matrix from Par1 to ParR. The call format is,

```
*MFUN, ParR,Func,Parl
```

Where,

Func: COPY or TRAN

*MFOURI calculates coefficients for, or evaluates, a series. It is used in performing harmonic analyses. The call format is,

```
*MFUN,Oper,COEFF,MODE,ISYM,THETA,CURVE
```

Where,

Oper: FIT, to calculate coefficients, or EVAL to evaluate curve.

7.19 *MOPER

The *MOPER command performs so many operations on matrix arrays that it deserves its own section. It can be used to do math, solve equations, do matrix operations, mapping, and node searching.

The call format is,

```
*MOPER,ParR,Parl,Oper,Par2,Par3,kDim,,kOut,LIMIT
```

Oper is the key argument in the command and it is used to really change the command into one of its forms.

Oper = INVERT

This inverts the matrix Par1 and places it in ParR:

```
*dim,a,,2,2
*dim,ainv,,2,2
a(1,1) = 4,3
```

```
a(1,2) = 3,2
```

This takes the matrix $\begin{bmatrix} 4 & 3 \\ 3 & 2 \end{bmatrix}$ and inverts it to: $\begin{bmatrix} -2 & 3 \\ 3 & -4 \end{bmatrix}$

Oper = MULT

This multiplies Par1 by Par2 and places the results in ParR. As you would expect, the number of rows in Par2 must equal the number or columns in Par1.

As an example:

```
*dim,a,,2,2
*dim,b,,2,2
*dim,c,,2,2
a(1,1) = 4,3
a(1,2) = 3,2
b(1,1) = 7,9
b(1,2) = -2,-6
*moper,c,a,mult,b
```

Is the same as: $\begin{bmatrix} 4 & 3 \\ 3 & 2 \end{bmatrix}\begin{bmatrix} 7 & -2 \\ 9 & -6 \end{bmatrix} = \begin{bmatrix} 55 & 39 \\ -26 & -18 \end{bmatrix}$

Oper = COVAR

This is a function used in statistics and it calculates the variance and covariance of the data stored in each column of Par1. It first places a mean vector in Par2, which contains the mean value of each column in Par1. Then the covariance values are calculated and placed in the off diagonal terms of ParR and the variance values in the diagonal. It is somewhat unique for an APDL command in that Par2 is an output variable name in this case.

As an example:

```
*dim,a,,2,2
*dim,b,,2,2
*dim,c,,2,2
a(1,1) = 4,7
a(1,2) = 3,-1
*moper,c,a,covar,b
```

Is the same as:

Input of A = $\begin{bmatrix} 4 & 3 \\ 7 & -1 \end{bmatrix}$

Mean Vector is put in B = $\begin{bmatrix} 5.5 \\ 1 \end{bmatrix}$

and the covariance matrix C = $\begin{bmatrix} 4.5 & -6 \\ -6 & 8 \end{bmatrix}$

Oper = CORR

This is another function used for statistical reduction of data. It calculates the correlation between the columns in the array Par1. Like Oper=COVAR it first places the mean values of each column in Par2, then it places the correlation coefficients in the off diagonal terms of ParR, putting 1 in for the diagonal terms.

As an example

```
*dim,a,,2,2
*dim,b,,2,2
*dim,c,,2,2
a(1,1)  = 4,7
a(1,2)  = 3,-1
*moper,c,a,corr,b
```

Is the same as:

Input of A = $\begin{bmatrix} 4 & 3 \\ 7 & -1 \end{bmatrix}$

Mean Vector is put in B = $\begin{bmatrix} 5.5 \\ 1 \end{bmatrix}$

and the correlation matrix C = $\begin{bmatrix} 1 & -1 \\ -1 & 1 \end{bmatrix}$

Oper = SOLVE

This is a simple and quick way to solve a set of simultaneous equations. Given a set of equations:

$$a_{11}x + a_{12}y + \cdots + a_{1n}m = b_1$$

$$a_{21}x + a_{22}y + \cdots + a_{2n}m = b_2$$

$$\cdots$$

$$a_{n1}x + a_{n2}y + \cdots + a_{nn}m = b_n$$

You place the values for [a] in Par1 and (b) in Par2 and the result for x, y, … m are placed in ParR.

As an example, take the equations:

$$x + y - z = 1$$

$$8x + 3y - 6z = 1$$

$$-4x - y + 3z = 1$$

To solve this you would use:

```
*dim,a,,3,3
*dim,b,,3
*dim,c,,3
a(1,1) = 1, 8, -4
a(1,2) = 1,3,-1
a(1,3) = -1,-6,3
b(1) = 1,1,1
*moper,c,a,solve,b
```

And the result for C = 2, 3, 4

Oper = SORT

This is a very useful command, but can be a bit confusing. The basic idea behind it is that you have a matrix in Par1 that you want to sort. You can specify a vector as Par2 and all the rows in Par1 will be rearranged in the same way that you need to rearrange the rows in Par2. The resulting sorted matrix is rewritten in Par1. This is not normal for APDL, so if you need your original matrix operate on a copy (*MFUN,ParR,COPY,Par1). ParR actually contains the new order of the old row numbers.

As an example:

```
*dim,a,,3,3
*dim,b,,3
*dim,c,,3
a(1,1) = 1, 8, -4
a(1,2) = 1,3,-1
a(1,3) = -1,-6,3
b(1) = 3,2,1
*moper,c,a,sort,b
```

Does a row sort on $\begin{bmatrix} 1 & 1 & -1 \\ 8 & 3 & -6 \\ -4 & -1 & 3 \end{bmatrix}$ using $\begin{bmatrix} 3 \\ 2 \\ 1 \end{bmatrix}$ as the sort key.

You end up with a $= \begin{bmatrix} -4 & -1 & 3 \\ 8 & 3 & -6 \\ 1 & 1 & -1 \end{bmatrix}$ and c $= \begin{bmatrix} 3 \\ 2 \\ 1 \end{bmatrix}$

But that is not all. If you want to sort on the values in the columns in your matrix, or if you want to have multiple sorting keys, you can leave Par2 blank and use the n1,n2,n3 arguments to specify the column number in the *MOPER command:

```
*MOPER,ParR,Par1,SORT,Par2,n1,n2,n3
```

In the previous example, we can sort on column 3 with:

```
*moper,c,a,sort,,3
```

and you get:

a $= \begin{bmatrix} 8 & 3 & -6 \\ 1 & 1 & -1 \\ -4 & -1 & 3 \end{bmatrix}$ and c $= \begin{bmatrix} 2 \\ 1 \\ 3 \end{bmatrix}$

Oper = NNEAR

This really is not a matrix function. It is a way to find the nodes closest to a list of X,Y,Z coordinates. To use it, you fill Par1 with the X, Y, Z points you want to find nodes close to. You can specify a tolerance for Par2. By default, Toler is 1. The node number for the closest node to the location on each row, is stored in the corresponding row in the ParR vector.

Oper = ENEAR

This works just like NNEAR, except it returns the element number for each element whose centroid is closest to the X, Y, Z position of each row, within the specified tolerance.

Oper = MAP

This is the most powerful, and the most complex operation for the *MOPER command. It is used to interpolate values from one set of points in 3D space (source) onto another set of points in 3D space (target). It is most commonly used to interpolate loads from one solution onto the nodes or element faces of another.

It looks like this:

```
*MOPER, ParR, Par1, MAP, Par2, Par3, kDim, --, kOut, LIMIT)
```

Par1 is an n x 3 array that contains the X, Y, Z coordinates that you want to interpolate on to, the targets. Where n is the number of target points.

Par2 is an m x i array that contains the source values you are interpolating. Where m is the number of source points and i is the number of values you want interpolated. You can have as many value columns as you want. This allows you to store maybe the X, Y, and Z values of a load in one array, rather than three separate.

Par3 is an m x 3 array that contains the X, Y, Z coordinates for your source values. Where m is the number of source points.

ParR is an n x m array that will therefore contain the resulting values for each column in Par2, interpolated onto the points in Par1.

It is helpful to understand the process that is used to do the mapping. For each point in the target array, the program finds a certain number of source points that are closest to that target point. The default is 20. It then looks at every combination of 3 (for 2d) or 4 (for 3d) points and builds a triangle or tetrahedral with them. And it finds the smallest one that contains the target node. Once it has those 3 or 4 source points that best surround the target, it linearly interpolates a value from those corner points.

The other three arguments to the command are important. If kDim = 2 or 0, then the program does a 2D interpolation. This is perfect for mapping surface loads. In essence it finds three source points around a given target point that form the smallest triangle around the target point and interpolate from those. If kDim = 3, then it works in 3D space and finds the smallest tetrahedral made of source points around the target points.

The kOut argument determines what the program does with target points that sit outside the source point cloud. If kOut = 0, the default, it uses the value of the nearest source point to the target point. If kOut = 1, then it simply sets the values on outside points to zero.

The last argument, LIMIT, sets the number of source points that the program looks at before it starts trying to build triangles or tetrahedral. The default of 20 is good, but you can really speed up your mapping if you make the number smaller. If your target or source points are irregularly distributed, you may need to raise LIMIT.

7.20   Workshop 7: Using Arrays and Tables

In this workshop you will modify the bracket6ws.mac macro (available with the inputs and demos files) to apply and solve two load steps. The first load step consists of downward force in the y-direction plus thermal expansion due to temperatures applied as a function of geometry. The second consists solely of varying pressures applied to the top surface of the bracket. After solving, we will use array operations to add the y-direction displacements between load cases (this can also be done with load case superposition as well) and calculate the maximum y-displacement resulting from the combined loads. We will also display the model name and the user login ID in the title.

1: Add `/INQUIRE` statements after the `/PREP7` command to retrieve the jobname and working directory and display them in the title.

```
/INQUIRE,job,JOBNAME
/INQUIRE,userid,LOGIN
/TITLE,File %job(1)% last modified by %userid(1)%
```

2: Using the following table, apply an X-Y temperature distribution to be effective for all load cases. Use the BF command to apply temperatures to nodes. You can try to define the table on your own, or use the code below.

		Y				
		0	0.25H	0.5H	0.75H	H
	0	600	480	390	300	240
X	0.60W	540	420	360	240	210
	0.85W	450	360	270	210	150
	W	300	210	180	120	60

These commands can be used between the lines `ALLSEL,ALL` and `FINISH` to build the table.

```
*DIM,TEMPTAB,TABLE,4,5,,X,Y
*TAXIS,TEMPTAB(1,0),1,0,.6*W,.85*W,W
*TAXIS,TEMPTAB(0,1),2,0,0.25*H,0.5*H,0.75*H,H
TEMPTAB(1,1)=600,540,450,300
TEMPTAB(1,2)=480,420,360,210
TEMPTAB(1,3)=390,360,270,180
TEMPTAB(1,4)=300,240,210,120
TEMPTAB(1,5)=240,210,150,60

BF,ALL,TEMP,%TEMPTAB%
```

Suggestion: Debug at this point by placing a `/EOF` after the `BF`, running the macro, then turning structural temperature contours on (`/PBF,TEMP,,1`) and plotting elements to verify that temperature has been applied correctly.

3: To write the first load step, insert the command `LSWRITE,1` after the `BF,…` command.

4: Insert commands to delete the forces and structural temperatures after load step 1 is written.

```
FDEL,ALL,ALL
BFDEL,ALL,ALL
```

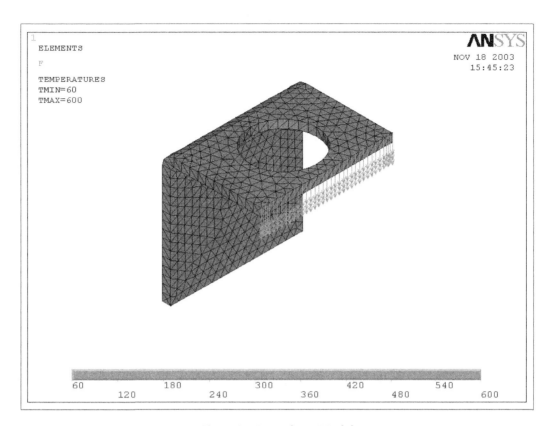

ELEMENTS

F

TEMPERATURES
TMIN=60
TMAX=600

ANSYS

NOV 18 2003
15:45:23

60 120 180 240 300 360 420 480 540 600

Figure 7.14: Loads on Model

5: Next we want to apply the table of pressure coefficients as shown below (OFFST=Rb+T). Based on these coefficients and a maximum pressure of 50 psi, apply a variable pressure along the top face of the bracket.

Table 7.2

		Z		
		0	0.4D	D
	OFFST	0.1	0.15	0.09
	OFFST+0.3(W-OFFST)	0.3	0.4	0.5
X	OFFST+0.75(W-OFFST)	0.9	1.0	0.8
	W	0.5	0.75	0.45

To do so, the following commands should be used after the BFDEL,ALL,ALL:

```
PMAX=50
OFFST=Rb+T
*DIM,PRESTAB,TABLE,4,3,,X,Z
*TAXIS,PRESTAB(1,0),1,OFFST,OFFST+.3*(W-OFFST),OFFST+.75*(W-OFFST),W
*TAXIS,PRESTAB(0,1),2,0,0.4*D,D
PRESTAB(1,1)=.1,.3,.9,.5
```

```
PRESTAB(1,2)=.15,.4,1,.75
PRESTAB(1,3)=.09,.5,.8,.45
!Convert pressure coefficients to absolute pressures
*TOPER,PRESTAB(1,1),PRESTAB(1,1),ADD,PRESTAB(1,1),PMAX,0,0
```

Then add this code to apply the pressure load along the top area:

```
ASEL,,LOC,Y,H
NSLA,,1
SF,ALL,PRES,%PRESTAB%
ALLSEL
```

6: Initially, the graphics don't show the pressure distributions when you turn on the pressure contours or arrows using `/PSF,PRESS,1` or `/PSF,PRESS,2` (they will display after the model is solved). In order to verify that the pressures were applied accurately, list the pressures at specific nodes by executing `SFLIS,P`. The four corners of the upper area are adequate for this workshop.

7: Write the second load step and solve both load steps by inserting the following after `ALLSEL`:

```
LSWRITE,2
LSSOLVE,1,2
```

8: Use vector operations to superimpose the y-displacements at each node for both load steps and obtain the maximum resulting deflection. Display this result to the user. The commands for doing so are as follows (insert after `LSSOLVE,1,2`):

```
FINI
/POST1              !Enter General Postprocessor

!Store y-deflections for each load step in a separate array
*GET,NUMNODE,NODE,,COUNT      !Obtain the number of nodes
*DO,k,1,2
    SET,k,1                   !Read in load step k
    *DIM,uy_ls%k%,,NUMNODE    !%k% substitutes value for
    *VGET,uy_ls%k%(1),NODE,1,U,Y  !k in parameter names
*ENDDO

!Add displacement vectors together
*DIM,uy_total,,NUMNODE
*VOPER,uy_total(1),uy_ls1(1),ADD,uy_ls2(1)

!Obtain max total displacement and display to user
*VABS,0,1 !UYs are negative but we want absolutes
*VSCFUN,uy_max,MAX,uy_total(1)
*MSG,UI,uy_max
```

```
Maximum total displacement = %G
```

2. Save file as bracket7.mac and execute.
3. You can display the pressure contours from the second load step by reading the results in using /POST1 and then SET,LAST and turning the pressure arrows (Utility Menu > PlotCtrls > Symbols; [PSF] = Pressures, Arrows) and numerical values (Utility Menu > PlotCtrls > Numbering; SVAL = On).

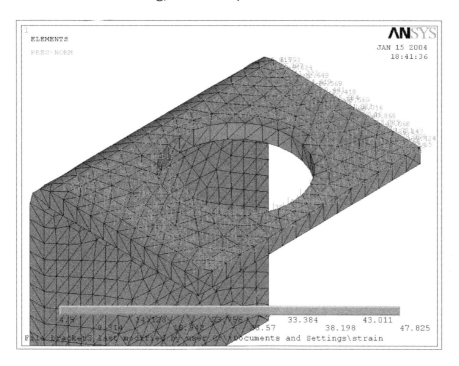

Figure 7.15: Resulting Loads

END OF WORKSHOP

Chapter 8: Importing and Exporting Data

8.1 Introduction

In previous chapters we have covered how to extract and manipulate large amounts of data using APDL. In this chapter we will look at how you can import data from outside of the program, and also export data, using formatting, to text files. This is a very important skill and when mastered, can make a significant difference in the effectiveness of ANSYS Mechanical and Mechanical APDL because it allows you to now connect the program to other programs in an easy, efficient, and automated manner.

8.2 Writing Data to Files

Data can be written to a text file using `*VWRITE` or `*MWRITE`. The `*VWRITE` command is a more general, and commonly used approach which can write out array data as well as scalar values, constants, and headings to a text file. `*MWRITE`, on the other hand, is used specifically to write out a matrix to a text file. Both commands require subsequent data format descriptors on the line beneath them.

NOTE: Any of the commands covered in this chapter that use a format statement of any kind cannot be pasted or typed in to the command line. They must be read from a file using /inp or as a macro that is executed.

8.3 *CFOPEN and *CFCLOSE

If you remember the part very early in this guide where creating macros from within a macro was discussed, you will remember the *CFOPEN and *CFCLOSE commands. The original use for these commands was to specify an output file and tell the program to open that file for writing. Then *CFCLOSE was used to close the file when you were done.

You also use these two commands to open a text file for writing out data.

```
*CFOPEN,file,ext,,Loc.
```

If this command is not used, the `*VWRITE` command defaults to writing to the output file (jobname.out). You control whether the data is appended to an existing file with or not with the Loc option. The default, blank, is to overwrite an existing file. If you specify APPEND, the data will be appended.

When you are done writing to the file, you need to close it with *CFCLOSE. Back in the day, you needed to do this just to be able to look at the file, it would be locked until the program exited or the file was closed. In modern operating systems you can usually look at the file from an editor without the close, but all of the data may not be in the file. ANSYS MAPDL does use buffering on I/O. So some data may be in memory waiting to be written, and the *CFCLOSE command dumps that data to the file and makes it available.

Note: *CFCLOSE is no longer documented in the help. But it is still a good idea to use it.

8.4   *VWRITE

*VWRITE writes data to a file in a formatted sequence with the call:

```
*VWRITE,Par1,Par2,Par3,…,Par19
```

Where,

- Par1 through Par19 are parameters or constants
- If the keyword SEQU is substituted for a parameter value, a sequence of numbers starting from 1 will be written for that item

If you are writing an array, you have to give the starting index for the array. The program will loop from the starting index, incrementing by one, to the end of the longest array, or to the value of *VLEN if it was specified in the previous line. If the array is multi-dimensional, only the first index (the row) is incremented and you need to specify the columns or plains.

*VMASK also can be used to skip certain rows in an array.

If a constant is specified for Par1 through Par19, that constant is written on every line.

The line after the *VWRITE command must be a format data descriptor. See the examples below for more information.

8.5   Format Data Descriptors

You have the choice of using either a FORTRAN or 'C' descriptor to format your output. In most cases the 'C' descriptors are going to provide greater flexibility and options. But if you are more comfortable with FOTRAN, or if you are working with an older macro, that may be the best way to go.

FOTRAN Descriptors

The *VWRITE line should be immediately followed by a line of format data descriptors. The most common format syntax used is FORTRAN. If FORTRAN is used, the data descriptor line should be enclosed in parentheses. Some of the FORTRAN data descriptors include:

nFw.d for floating point format	w = column width
nEw.d for scientific notation	d = number of decimal places
nAw for characters (not string)	n = number of occurrences
nX for blank spaces	

All of the FORTRAN descriptors for *real* numbers will work with APDL. In addition you can use (A) for strings up to 8 characters long. The (X) works for blanks. As with any FORTRAN descriptor, you have to use parenthesis around the descriptors.

The Integer (I) and open-format (*) descriptors DO NOT work with APDL. Many an hour has been spent by users trying to get an integer or open-format to work with APDL. If you need to write an integer or a string longer than 8 characaters, uses the 'C' format descriptors.

In addition to the descriptors, you can specify text to be written to every line by simply putting the string, up to 8 characters long, in single quotes: `('This is a Node:", 4F12.6)`

If you see a collection of #'s in your output file, the item you are trying to print will not fit in the space provided by the descriptor. You usually need to raise w.

There are two undocumented descriptors that come in very handy that should be mentioned because they deal with suppressing or inserting a new line (what we used to call linefeed or carriage return):

$	Suppress new line
/	Insert new line

Use the '/' to avoid a *VWRITE that simply puts in a blank line and use '/' to make your macro more generic so that you can use *DO loops to deal with a different number of items to be printed on a given line. See the example below to get a better feel for how these work.

'C' Descriptors

You can also use a subset of the standard 'C' descriptors. When using these, do not enclose them in parenthesis. This is how APDL tells if it is FORTRAN or 'C'.

Some of the C data descriptors include:

- %wI for integer data
- %0wI for integers padded with 0's
- %w.pE for engineering notation of a real number
- %w.pG for general numeric format
- %w.pF for a floating point number
- %wC for an alphanumeric string (128 character max)
- %-wC for a left justified alphanumeric string (128 character max)
- %wX for w blank characters
- %% for a single percent sign
- %/ for a line break

Unlike FORTRAN, there is no 'n' descriptor to repeat a given format. So if you need four numbers of the same type you have to repeat the same descriptor four times.

In addition to the descriptors, the 'C' format will print out any text you specify on the line that is not part of a descriptor: This is a Node: %8I %F12.6 %F12.6 %f12.6

8.6   *VWRITE Examples

To illustrate how this works, here are some examples.

Remember – you cannot paste commands like *vwrite that have format statements. You must read them from a file or execute a macro.

First, we need to create some dummy arrays. This code randomly fills a deflection array and then calculates the total deflection:

```
finish
/clear
/prep7
*dim,u_comp,,10,2
*dim,u_total,,10
*dim,t1,,10
*dim,t2,,10
*vfill,u_comp(1,1),rand,0,.03
*vfill,u_comp(1,2),rand,-.124,.04
*voper,t1(1),u_comp(1,1),mult,u_comp(1,1)
*voper,t2(1),u_comp(1,2),mult,u_comp(1,2)
*voper,u_total(1),t1(1),add,t2(1)
*vfun,u_total(1),sqrt,u_total(1
```

Now that we have the arrays, we can write out the results:

```
*cfopen,deflections,txt
*vwrite
('Node','   ','UX',5X,'UY',7X,'USUM')
*vwrite,sequ,u_comp(1,1),u_comp(1,2),u_total(1)
(F4.0,3F8.4)
*cfclose
```

This gives:

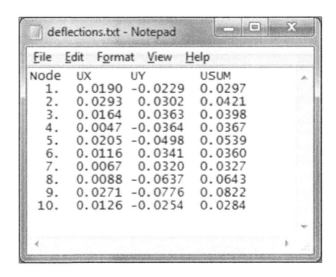

Figure 8.1: Output from *VWRITE

Your values will be different because the UX and UY values are randomly generated. But it should look the same.

Looking at the code you can see that the first thing you do is open a file to write into with *CFOPEN. Next you need to write the header. This is not from an array so you simply put the text you want written in a FORTRAN statement, with the strings enclosed in single quotes and separated by commas.

Then in the next line is a *VWRITE for the actual data. You specify the starting row (1) and the column for each coordinate (1=x, 2=y). Because we do not have an array of node numbers, and our numbers go from 1 to 10, we simply use the sequ command to specify the node numbers.

The FOTRAN format data descriptor is next. It prints the node number as a float, then the displacements. Then you close the file.

The example above can be slightly modified to put a blank line before and after the header, by using the / descriptor:

```
*cfopen,deflections,txt
*vwrite
(/,'Node','   ','UX',5X,'UY',7X,'USUM',/)
*vwrite,sequ,u_comp(1,1),u_comp(1,2),u_total(1)
(F4.0,3F8.4)
*cfclose
```

This gives the same thing, but with spaces above and below the header:

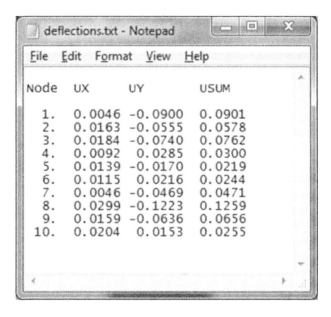

Figure 8.2: Output from *VWRITE, with Spaces on Header

Ignoring that change, the same thing using a 'C' format would be:

```
*cfopen,deflections,txt
*vwrite
Node    UX          UY          USUM
*vwrite,sequ,u_comp(1,1),u_comp(1,2),u_total(1)
%4i %8.4f %8.4f %8.4f
*cfclose
```

And the result would be:

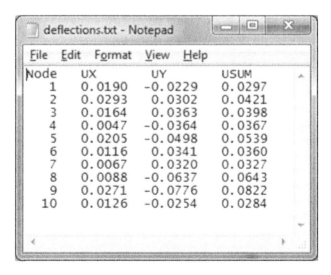

Figure 8.3: Output from *VWRITE using 'C' Formats

Note the differences in the output. The node number is an actual integer. There are also extra spaces between the columns because there were spaces in the format.

This next example shows the use of the SEQU argument, writing the same text to every line, and writing a constant:

```
*cfopen,totaldef,txt
*vwrite,sequ,u_total(1), 3.14159
('Total deflection at node',F4.0,' ','=',' ',F6.4,' And Pi = ',F6.4)
*cfclose
```

Gives,

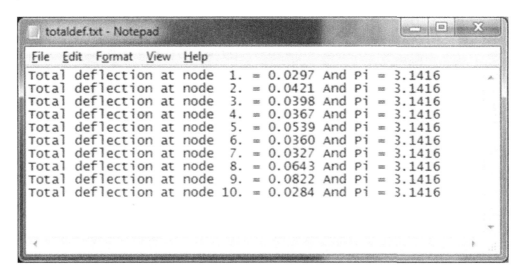

Figure 8.4: Output from *VWRITE using SEQU Argument

This example shows the use of masking and length control. Using the same arrays, we want to write out every other node from 3 to 6. So you would start at row 3, and go 4 spaces. To skip every other row, use a mask array of alternating 0's and 1's. The other thing we need to take care of is the fact that our node number is not simply 1 to 10. Now we need a node number array, and we will use *vfill to create it:

```
*dim,vmsk,,10    ! An array for our mask
*dim,ndnm,,10    ! A node number array
vmsk(1) = 1,0,1,0,1,0,1,0,1,0 ! fill the mask array.
*vfill,ndnm(1),ramp,1,1    ! fill the node number array
*cfopen,shortdef,txt
*vwrite
Node   UX        UY        USUM
*vlen,4               !specify the length
*vmask,vmsk(3)        !specify the mask
*vwrite,ndnm(3),u_comp(3,1),u_comp(3,2),u_total(3)
%4i %8.4f %8.4f %8.4f
*cfclose
```

This produces:

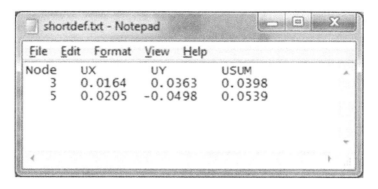

Figure 8.5: Output from *VWRITE using *VMASK

The last example shows a generic routine for writing out 2D tables of any size. It takes the name of the table to write and the name of the file to write to as arguments. It uses FORTRAN format statements so that we can leverage the '$' descriptor and write out one column at a time for each row:

```
ttbl = arg1       ! Get the name of the table you want to write
fname = arg2      ! get the name of the file to write to

*get,nrw,parm,%ttbl%,dim,X        ! Get the size of the table
*get,ncl,parm,%ttbl%,dim,Y
*get,xax,parm,%ttbl%,var,1        ! Get the names of the columns
*get,yax,parm,%ttbl%,var,2

*cfopen,%fname%    !Open the file

*vwrite,ttbl,xax,yax    ! Write a header (note / to add a line)
('Table: ',A,' ',A,' vs ',A,/)

*vwrite  ! write 10 spaces, then don't write a new line by using $
('          |',$)

*do,jj,1,ncl ! Loop on each column, writing out the column
    *vlen,1
    *vwrite,%ttbl%(0,jj)
    (g10.4,$)
*enddo
*vwrite    !You need a line feed now, just write a space
(' ')
*vwrite  !Write a line of  dashes to separate the header, with a pipe
(10x,'|',$)    ! to separate the row values
*do,jj,1,ncl
    *vwrite
    (10('-'),$)
```

```
*enddo
*vwrite
(' ')
*do,ii,1,nrw     ! write the values, looping on row, then column
    *vlen,1
    *vwrite,%ttbl%(ii,0)
    (g10.4,'|',$)
    *do,jj,1,ncl
        *vlen,1
        *vwrite,%ttbl%(ii,jj)
        (g10.4,$)
    *enddo
    *vwrite
    (' ')
*enddo
*cfclose
```

If we put this macro into a file tlbltool.mac, we can build a sample table and display it with:

```
*dim,mycnv,table,3,3,,'RPM','X'
*taxis,mycnv(1,1),1,0,1000,.2001e8
*taxis,mycnv(1,1),2,0,1,2
mycnv(1,1)=.25,4,10
mycnv(1,2)=.35,7,15
mycnv(1,3)=.45,10,28
tbltool,'mycnv','foo9.txt'
*list,'foo9.txt'
```

This produces:

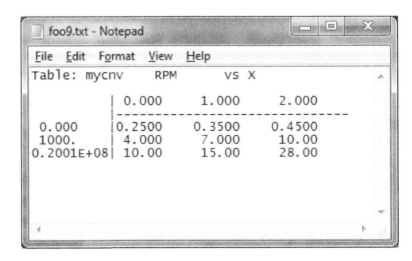

Figure 8.6: Example of Writing a Formatted Table

8.7   *MWRITE

The *VWRITE with the *CFOPEN/*CFCLOSE command is very flexible and it allows for some fairly sophisticated output. However, when you want to write out a single table or array, you can use the *MWRITE by itself to write the contents of single array or table parameter.

The call for *MWRITE is:

```
*MWRITE,ParR,file,ext,,label,n1,n2,n3

! ParR is the name of the array to be written
! file is the file name for the output file
! ext is the filename extension
! label defines the looping order for the right:
!    IJK, IKJ, JIK (default), JKI, KIJ, or KJI
! n1,n2,n3 is the max value to write for each I,J,K value
```

The line after *MWRITE must be a FORTRAN or 'C' format statement as described for *VWRITE.

Note two things about this command. First, the file name for the output file is specified in the command. You do not use *CFOPEN/*CFCLOSE. Second, the user specifies which indices to look on and that the default is not IJK but JIK. This is the biggest source of error for those using this command. Make sure you specify the order you want it to loop on.

Here is an example for the *MWRITE command.

First we want to define a simple 2D table:

Table 8.1: Sample Pressure Table

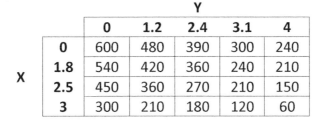

		Y				
		0	1.2	2.4	3.1	4
	0	600	480	390	300	240
X	1.8	540	420	360	240	210
	2.5	450	360	270	210	150
	3	300	210	180	120	60

Use the following commands

```
*DIM,TMPTAB,TABLE,4,5,,X,Y
*TAXIS,TMPTAB(1,1),1,0,1.8,2.5,3
*TAXIS,TMPTAB(1,1),2,0,1.2,2.4,3.1,4
TMPTAB(1,1)=600,540,450,300
```

```
TMPTAB(1,2)=480,420,360,210
TMPTAB(1,3)=390,360,270,180
TMPTAB(1,4)=300,240,210,120
TMPTAB(1,5)=240,210,150,60
```

Then use *MWRITE to print it to a file

```
*mwrite,tmptab(1,1),prs1,txt  !Default JIK order
(5F6.1)
```

Produces:

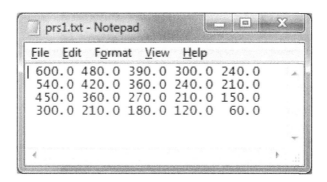

Figure 8.7: Example of *MWRITE with Default JIK Order

If we specify the order as IJK, we get:

```
*mwrite,tmptab(1,1),prs2,txt,,IJK
(5F6.1)
```

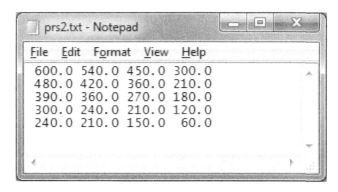

Figure 8.8: Example of *MWRITE with Default IJK Order

This shows why the default is JIK. You want to write out the values for a given row (I) on each line. Or in do loop language: The outer loop is I and the inner loop is j: for each row (I) write out the value in each column (J) then a line feed, then increment I.

Another way to look at it is to use the *VWRITE equivalent:

```
*cfopen,prs1_vw,txt
```

```
*vwrite,tmptab(1,1),tmptab(1,2),tmptab(1,3),tmptab(1,4),tmptab(1,5)
(5F6.1)
*cfclose
```

Produces:

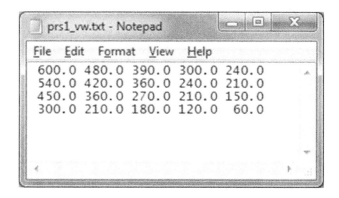

Figure 8.9: Example Output of a Table using *VWRITE

8.8   *VREAD

Just as *VWRITE is the most powerful tool for writing to files, *VREAD is the best for reading from files. However, it should be noted that *VREAD is not a "read" version of *VWRITE. It only allows you to read data into one array at a time. This means that the number of items per line, format, and data type cannot change in a file.

*VREAD reads arrays or matrices from a text file. The call format is,

```
*VREAD,ParR,file,ext,,LABEL,n1,n2,n3,NSKIP
```

Where:

- ParR is the name of the array to store the data in. It must be defined with *DIM
- File,ext refers to the file being read
- LABEL defines the order in which the text columns are read into array columns. Can be equal to (=) IJK (default), JIK, IKJ, JKI, KIJ, or KJI. LABEL must be defined when reading in a matrix, even if it is IJK.
- n1,n2,n3 are the sizes for I, J, and K.
- NSKIP is the number of lines to skip at the beginning of the file. Used to skip over headers.

*VREAD, just like *VWRITE, requires a subsequent line of FORTRAN format descriptors. The descriptors must be for real numbers or character strings.

nFw.d for floating point format   w = column width

nEw.d for scientific notation   d = number of decimal places

nAw for characters (not string)   n = number of occurrences

nX for blank spaces

Note that the A descriptor can only read 8 characters. Use *SREAD if you need more.

Here are some examples to demonstrate the use of *VREAD:

If we have a text file that looks like this:

Figure 8.10: Sample Text File with Columns of Numbers

In order to read just the first column, we create an array that is four items long and read the file with *VREAD:

```
*dim,presstab,,4
*vread,presstab(1,1),pressure,txt
(F6.1)
```

This Produces:

Array Parameter PRESSTAB	
	1
1	5
2	15
3	45
4	25

Figure 8.11: Array Resulting from *VREAD

If we want all of the columns, we need to specify a 2D array of the right size and specify how many rows and columns:

```
*dim,presstab,,3,4
*vread,presstab(1,1),pressure,txt,,ijk,3,4
(3F6.1)
```

Which creates:

Array Parameter PRESSTAB	1	2	3	4
1	5	15	45	25
2	7.5	20	50	37.5
3	4.5	25	40	22.5

Figure 8.12: 2D Array *VREAD Example, IJK Order

Notice how the rows and columns are switched. That is because we used the IJK order.

In order to match things up, we need to use the JIK order:

```
*dim,presstab,,4,3
*vread,presstab(1,1),pressure,txt,,jik,3,4
(3F6.1)
```

Produces:

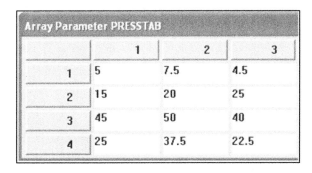

Array Parameter PRESSTAB	1	2	3
1	5	7.5	4.5
2	15	20	25
3	45	50	40
4	25	37.5	22.5

Figure 8.13: 2D Array *VREAD Example, JIK Order

8.9   *TREAD

The fact that a table has to have indices defined you really cannot use *VREAD to read in a table. *TREAD solves this problem by knowing what a table is and how to read it:

The syntax for the command is:

```
*TREAD,ParR,file,ext,,NSKIP
```

Where:

- ParR is the name of the array to store the data in. It must be defined with *DIM
- File,ext refers to the file being read
- NSKIP defines the number of lines to skip at the beginning of the file. Use this to skip headers.

No format descriptors are necessary and text must be tab delimited, comma delimited, or space delimited. As a note, Excel can save in all three formats under File > Save as...

*TREAD assumes that the first row contains the row index values and that the first column contains the column index values. The (0,0) position is ignored, but putting a 0 in there is a good idea.

Here is a simple example. Given the following text file:

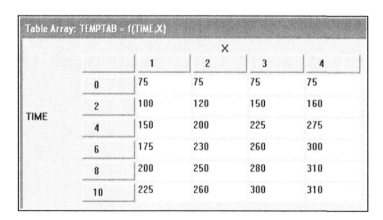

Figure 8.14: Sample Text File with Tabular Data

Use this code to read it in:

```
*dim,temptab,table,6,4,,TIME,X
*tread,temptab(0,0),temptable,txt,,3
```

Notice the 3 for NSKIP in order to skip over the header

The following table is produced:

Table Array: TEMPTAB = f(TIME,X)

TIME		X			
		1	2	3	4
	0	75	75	75	75
	2	100	120	150	160
	4	150	200	225	275
	6	175	230	260	300
	8	200	250	280	310
	10	225	260	300	310

Figure 8.15: Results from *TREAD

8.10 *SREAD

All of the previous commands used for reading data into MAPDL are focused on placing the data into a parameter or array of the proper type: character, number, or table. There is one more command that simply places whatever is in your file into a string array: *SREAD.

The syntax for the command is:

```
*SREAD, StrArray, Fname, Ext, --, nChar, nSkip, nRead
```

Where:

- StrArray is the name of the string array. You do not have to dimension it up front, the command will create the array with nChar characters per row and nRead rows.
- Fname, Ext refers to the file being read
- nChar is the number of characters per line to read. It defaults to the number of characters on the longest line in the file.
- nSkip defines the number of lines to skip at the beginning of the file. Use this to skip headers.
- nRead is the number of lines to read. The default is to read the whole file.

There are two primary uses for this command. The first is documentation. You can use it to read in some piece of information that you want to store with your model, but that you do not need to actually access and use. Say a test report or the background information on where your material properties came from. We have also seen people document their whole simulation process in a text file then *SREAD it in so it will be in the database.

The second, and more common use, is to read text into a macro that then uses the string function commands to parse the contents of a file, and then do things with it. There really is no limit to how this can be applied and it makes APDL a very powerful language for reading in information.

As an example, assume you have an in-house program that generates material properties from a database, but it outputs them in its own unique format of: matProp(matnum,value). A data file may look like:

```
youngmod(2,32.345e6)
poisson(2,.23)
density(2,0.00034)
```

You could use this macro to read the file and create material properties:

```
*sread,matstuff,mymat,txt,,
*get,nln,parm,matstuff,dim,2

*do,i,1,nln
    p = '('
    kwend = strpos(matstuff(1,i),p)
    cm1 = strpos(matstuff(1,i),',')
    len = strleng(matstuff(1,i))
    matprop = strsub(matstuff(1,i),1,kwend-1)
    matnum = valchr(strsub(matstuff(1,i),kwend+1,cm1-kwend-1))
    val = valchr(strsub(matstuff(1,i),cm1+1,len-cm1-1))
    *if,matprop,eq,'youngmod',then
        mp,ex,matnum,val
    *endif
    *if,matprop,eq,'poisson',then
        mp,nuxy,matnum,val
    *endif
    *if,matprop,eq,'density',then
        mp,dens,matnum,val
    *endif
*enddo
```

You could of course do this faster with python or many other languages, even Excel. But sometimes you want to have all of your code in APDL and *SREAD provides a lot of options.

8.11   Reading Data as a Macro

The most robust way to read data in to Mechanical APDL is to use an external program to convert the data into actual APDL commands. Instead of trying to read numbers into a parameter or into an array, simply write out the data as a parameter or an array. This avoids any formatting problems, read errors, and makes things very general. The down side is that it requires programming outside of APDL.

8.12   Importing to POST26 Using Tcl

The Variable Viewer in the Time History processor has a button for importing data as shown:

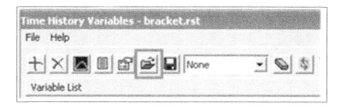

Figure 8.16: POST26 Variable Viewer

This was created to allow people to quickly read external data into POST26 so that it could be compared to data generated in ANSYS. It places the information into a POST26 variable, but it can be transferred into an array.

The Import Data button executes two Tcl commands, which can also be included in batch script:

- ~eui, 'ansys::results::timeHist::TREAD directorypath/filename arrayname' reads data from filename located under directorypath and automatically defines, dimensions, and fills arrayname with that data (no *DIM necessary).

- The data contained in arrayname is then placed into a variable by issuing ~eui,'ansys::results::timeHist::vputData arrayname variablenumber'

8.13   Workshop 8: Importing and Exporting Data

In this workshop we will modify bracket7.mac to import the temperature and pressure tables from existing text files rather than define them manually. We will also write out the maximum displacement and displacement arrays to a text file.

1: Make sure that temperatures.txt and prescoefs.txt are in your working directory. You can find these files in the 'inputs and demos' folder that accompanies the training material.

2: Copy bracket7.mac to bracket8.mac and open with a text editor.   Delete the TEMPTAB array parameter definitions and replace them with the line (insert after the *DIM command):

```
*TREAD,TEMPTAB(0,0),temperatures,txt,,3
```

```
temperatures.txt - Notepad
File  Edit  Format  View  Help
Applied Temperatures vs. Location

X-Loc     Y-Location
0         0        1        2        3        4
0         600      480      390      300      240
1.8       540      420      360      240      210
2.55      450      360      270      210      150
3         300      210      180      120      60
```

Figure 8.17: Contents of temperatures.txt File

(It's a good idea to add /EOF after the *TREAD line and run the macro to make sure the table is defined correctly)

3: Delete the line OFFST=Rb+T since it is no longer needed.

4: Delete the PRESTAB array parameter definitions and replace them with the following line (insert after *DIM and before the *TOPER line).

```
*TREAD,PRESTAB(0,0),prescoefs,txt,,3
```

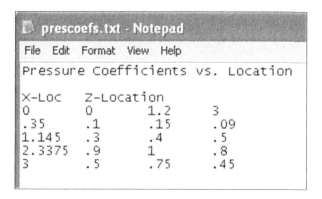

Figure 8.18: Contents of prescoefs.txt File

(It's a good idea to run the macro with /EOF after the *TREAD line, then again after the *TOPER line, to make sure the table is defined correctly)

5: Delete the *MSG command and the subsequent line and replace with the following:

```
*CFOPEN,displacements,txt
*VWRITE,uy_max
('Maximum total displacement = ',F6.4)
*VWRITE
(' ')
*VWRITE
('Nodal Displacements')
*VWRITE
```

```
(' ')
*VWRITE
('Node',2X,'Load Step 1',2X,'Load Step 2',2X,'LS1 + LS2')
*VWRITE,SEQU,uy_ls1(1),uy_ls2(1),uy_total(1)
(F7.0,2F13.4,F11.4)
*CFCLOSE
```

6: Save bracket8.mac and execute the macro.

7: Open the file displacements.txt and verify that the output looks as shown below

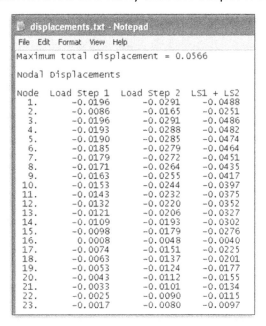

Figure 8.19: Correct Output from Workshop 8

Chapter 9:   Implementing Macros in a Work Group

When you start writing APDL macros you usually write short little scripts that you use yourself. As you get better, you start sharing them with other users, and before you know it you are making macros that many people want to use. Sending them around in email works for a while, but at some point you need to develop some methods to control their use and make sure people have easy access to them. This section will demonstrate how macros can be implemented in a work group.

9.1   Sharing Macros in Directories

Macros can be shared by multiple users by putting them in directories that ANSYS MAPDL searches in when it finds a command it does not recognize. If you have macros that you wish to share with users, you can place them in one of these directories on each machine, or in a shared directory that everyone has mounted on their machine. Either way ANSYS MAPDL will go through the directories in a specific order, and if it finds a filename.mac where filename matches the unknown command, it will execute that macro.

First Location:

It first looks in the APDL directory. This is where the macros that come with ANSYS MAPDL are stored and you can add your own macros into the directory. It is stored in the ANSYS product directory under: C:\Program Files\ANSYS Inc\vNNN\ansys\apdl for windows and /ansys_inc/vNNN/ansys/apdl for Linux, where NNN is the version number.

Second Location:

The program next looks at the environment variable ANSYS_MACROLIB and if there are directories in that variable, it checks them in the order specified. The environment variable should be set to a delimited list of full directory paths, where the syntax is a bit unique for Windows:

```
c:\dir1;d:\dir2;c:\dir3;k:\dir
```

The drive letter is given, followed by a colon, followed by the directory path. Each directory is separated by a semi-colon.

For Linux it is a bit easier, simply separate the directories (with trailing slash) with a colon:

```
dir/:dir2/:dir3/
```

Third Location:

The next place that ANSYS MAPDL looks is either in your home directory or in a directory you specify at run time with an APDL command /PSEARCH. If you do not use /PSEARCH, the default is your home directory. /PSEARCH takes a directory name as its only argument.

Fourth Location:

If a matching macro cannot be found in any of the locations listed above, ANSYS MAPDL simply looks in the current working directory. This is where most of us keep our macros, but it is not a good place for shared macros.

The /PSEARCH command has some other uses. /PSEARCH,OFF tells the program to only look in the ANSYS and current directories, skipping your home and any ANSYS_MACROLIB directories. /PSEARCH,STAT shows the searched directories.

9.2   Macro Libraries

A macro library is a single file containing multiple macros. Each macro starts with a MACRONAME, and ends with /EOF. Macro library can have any file name extension, up to 8 characters and should be placed in your macro search path. For example:

Figure 9.1: Example Macro Library

You access a macro library by specifying the library file using the *ULIB command. For example, to specify that macros are in the mymacros.mlib file, which resides in the d:/myaccount/macros directory, you would issue the following command:

```
*ulib,mymacros,mlib,d:/myaccount/macros/
```

After selecting a macro library, you can execute any macro contained in the library by specifying it through the *USE command. As with macros contained in individual files, you can specify arguments as parameters in the *USE command.

When you access a macro with *USE, the program actually makes a temporary file in your current working directory with the macro name specified, executes the macro, then deletes it. So your macro names must be valid as file names as well.

When you are done using a library, you should execute *ULIB with no arguments so that you can access other macros.

9.3   Encrypting Macros

To protect the contents of a macro for proprietary or other reasons, macros can be encrypted:

Create and debug the macro as usual. Add the /ENCRYPT command as the first and last lines of the macro. The /ENCRYPT command for the first line of the macro has the following syntax:

```
/ENCRYPT,Encryption_key,File_name,File_ext,Directory_Path/
```

Where

- *Encryption_key* is an eight-character password.
- *File_name* is the name of the encrypted macro filename.
- *File_ext* is an optional file extension for the encrypted macro file. If you want users to execute the macro as an "unknown" command, you should use the **.mac** extension.
- *Directory_Path/* is the optional directory path that can contain up to 60 characters; you only need this argument if you do not want to write the encrypted macro file to your "home" directory. You must make the "/" (or "\" for Windows systems) the final character of the path name (otherwise the last directory name is prepended to the file name).

As an example:

```
/encrypt,foobar,block_sphere_e,mac,
/nopr
/prep7
/view,,-1,-2,-3
block,,arg1,,arg2,,arg3
sphere,arg4
vsbv,1,2
/gopr finish
```

```
/encrypt
```

The file that is created should look like this:

```
/DECRYPT,foobar
01XOY.m
02nZ0`P.
03w4dEn;:ii/Zy$OJ
04~gOZz:h;u6x$NxYQBJ#(-R&
05nP_t"CddAP,
06Vjq&hi/_
07&v}NLC5Rf-,O
/DECRYPT
```

The /ENCRYPT command at the top of the macro instructs ANSYS to encrypt the file and use the string "mypasswd" is the encryption key. It will create an encrypted macro file called myenfile.mac and place it in the /macros subdirectory of the home directory. The /ENCRYPT command at the bottom instructs ANSYS to stop the encryption process and write the encrypted macro to the specified file.

You create the encrypted version of the macro by running the macro. This will create the encrypted file and place it in your directory. Now when you run the new file, ANSYS MAPDL will decrypt the file in memory and run it.

The encrypted macro contains a /NOPR (no print) command as its second line to turn off echoing of ANSYS commands to the session log file. This is important if you wish to prevent users from reading the contents of the macro from the session log. It's a good practice to reactivate the session log by issuing the /GOPR (go print) command as the last command in the macro before the ending /ENCRYPT command.

Keep the original file as a reference because there is no way to save a copy of the decrypted file.

Do note that this is not a very secure decryption and it should not be used for any information that you really need to protect. It is useful as a way to keep others from gaining access to your algorithms without a lot of effort. It is also useful as a way to keep users within your own organization from going in and hacking a macro and introducing problems. In large companies, this can be very useful.

Chapter 10:   Menu Customization Overview with UIDL

10.1   UIDL – The Menu and Dialog Language for ANSYS MAPDL

The menu system in ANSYS MAPDL is defined by a series of text files that use a proprietary language called UIDL – User Interface Design Language. The name is usually pronounced as "wee-del." The language is very concise, very fast, and platform independent. Newer users who are used to describing menu systems with XML or other very verbose markup languages may find the syntax a bit cryptic, but once a user takes the time to learn it, they quickly realize its power and speed.

With the use of the ANSYS MAPDL GUI becoming less and less frequent, the need and value of modifying the menu structure and adding your own commands into it is lessening. However, in some circumstances there is a need and value to do so.

10.2   The Menu Building Process

When the GUI for ANSYS MAPDL is started, the program reads a menulistNNN.ans file that is found in the ANSYS program directory under ansys/gui/en-us/UIDL. For different languages, the directory is different. This file is simply a list of the menu files that need to be read in order to build the menus. This makes it very easy for users to add their own menus to the ANSYS MAPDL GUI by making a new file, and adding it to the list.

At version 14.0 the file looks like this:

```
%ANSYS140_DIR%\gui\en-us\UIDL\UIMENU.GRN
%ANSYS140_DIR%\gui\en-us\UIDL\UIFUNC1.GRN
%ANSYS140_DIR%\gui\en-us\UIDL\UIFUNC2.GRN
%ANSYS140_DIR%\gui\en-us\UIDL\MECHTOOL.AUI
```

Each of the files defines a menu structure, dialog boxes, and some commands. They used to also describe the help system, but that has been replaced with a shared online help facility across all of the ANSYS products.

The program reads each file in turn and builds the menus and dialogs described within.

10.3   UIDL Control Files

The descriptions for the menu and functions are contained in Granule files, using the extension .GRN. Each file contains three parts:

- Header: Used by the program to figure out what is in the file
- Building Blocks: Defines GUI items
- Index: Added by the program when the file is read to speed access up. You put zeros in when you make a granule file and the program will fill them in at run time.

The three granule files that ANSYS MAPDL needs to run are:

- UIMENU.GRN Defines the GUI menus
- UIFUNC1.GRN Defines common commands in menus
- UIFUNC2.GRN Defines remaining commands in menus

Each line in a granule file has to be either a header command, a block command or an end command.

Header commands always start with a colon ":" and a single character. This is followed by a space and options that are specific to that command. There are three types of header commands: Control File Header, Menu Block Header, and Function Block Header.

Block commands are three letters, followed by an underscore "_", followed by a modifier.

The end command is simply :E END. Nothing that fancy, but it needs to be there to tell the program that the block is done.

10.3.1 UIDL Control File Header Commands

For the Control File Header, the first four lines in an granule file, you must use the following four commands in this order:

- :F filename
  Defines filename and must match the name of the file that contains the header

- :D description text
  This is a description for the file and should have key info you want to share

- :I   0,   0,   0
  The index line, put in zeros to get started. Index line used by ANSYS
  0's must be in columns 9, 18, and 27 followed by commas, except the last one

- :!
  A separator denoting the end of the header commands.

Here is what a sample Control File Header looks like for a custom menu file:

```
:F NEWMENU.GRN
:D New menu for PADT Custom ANSYS Commands
:I     0,     0,         0
:!
```

10.3.2 UIDL Menu Blocks

The user accesses commands through menus. These are windows that cascade in a tree like structure with either functions called out in them or child menus. You define a menu with a header that names and labels the menu, then block commands that specify either functions or other menus. You then finish up the block with the :E END command.

The commands for a menu header block are:

Command	Req.	Description	Example
:N Men_*String*	Yes	Defines Name of Menu to be *String*	Men_TimePost
:S 0, 0, 0	Yes	Index Place Holder for Block. 0's must be in columns 9, 16 and 23, followed by commas	
:T Menu	Yes	Tells ANSYS the Block Type is Menu	:T Menu
:A *String*	Yes	Specifies that the Text in the Parent Menu be set to *String*. A ">" is automatically appended. If it is pat of a sub-head, then indent by 3 spaces	
:D *String*	No	Describes the Block. Sort of a Comment	:D Time History Menu
:C *String*	No	Executes the ANSYS Command *String*. Can also call external libraries (~commands). Prefix *string* with ")" to hide commands from log file and start with :C)/nopr to turn of echo to output window.	:C *get,_z1,active,, routin
:K *Keyword_Logic*	No	Filters the Block Based on Keywords. See Appendix A of Programming Manual	:K #((PREP7*SOLUTION)+(CFD)
:P *Product_Logic*	No	Filters the Block Based Upon Product Codes See Appendix B of Programming Manual	:P (FLOTRAN)
:! *String*	No	Separator and Comments	:! Optional End of Block
:E END	Yes	Specifies the end of a block	: END

The first four commands are required and must be the first four lines of your block. You must also have the :E END at the end of your block. Most people also place a :! Comment after that in order to make the file more readable

Here is an example Menu Block Header:

```
:N Men_Mesh
:S    524,    323,    194
:T Menu
:A    Mesh
:D Mesh
:C )/NOPR
:C )
:C )*GET,_z1,ACTIVE,,KEYWORD,,MESHTOOL
:C )*IF,_z1,eq,1,THEN
:C )*create,ansuitmp
:C )*msg,note,
:C )Some functions of this menu cannot be used while the %/&
:C )MeshTool is active.
:C )*end
:C )/input,ansuitmp
:C )*ENDIF
:C )/GO
:K #(igesfail)
```

The name of the block is Men_Mesh and the Index was filled in by the program. The :T command tells the program that the type is a Menu and :A specifies the name that the user will see as Mesh, and the descriptor :D echoes that. Notice the spaces after the :A, these will show up in the menu when it is rendered and is a way to organize the look of your menus.

The next set of lines are very important. They are APDL commands imbedded into the menu that get executed when the menu is accessed. The same is true for Function Block Headers. In most cases you put checks in here to make sure it is OK to bring up the menu and maybe flash up a warning, as in this example.

Following the header are the menu block commands. There are only four and they specify another menu, a function, a horizontal line or a line of unelectable text, usually used as a sub-heading in a menu. The commands are:

Command	Description	Example
Men_String	Specifies a menu defined in another Menu Block to be inserted into this menu. String must match the String used in a :N command	Men_p26Settings
Fnc_String	Specifies a function defined in a Function block to be inserted into this menu. String must match the String used in a :N command	Fnc_nplot
Sep_	Inserts a Horizontal Separator Line	Sep_
String	A String by itself is placed in the menu as un-selectable text. It is used as a heading for sub-items. The String values on the :A for the items inserted under the heading should be indented 3 Spaces.	-Modeling-

The Fnc_ and Men_ commands use the same syntax. The name of the menu you want to show on the row is defined with a string. This is the string that you use with the :N command when you define the function or the menu. It is the pointer to what you want to display in the menu.

The program appends menu lines with a >, function that do not bring up a dialog with +, and functions that do bring up a dialog with ….

It is convention to put sub-headers between two dashes: -Areas-. It is also convention to use leading spaces to give some structure to the different levels within a menu.

Here is an example Mesh menu:

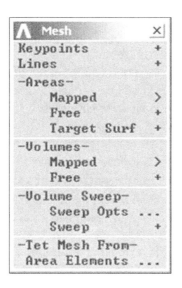

Figure 10.1: Mesh Menu

The file describing the menu, looks like this:

```
:N Men_Mesh
:S    524,   323,   194
:T Menu
:A    Mesh
:D Mesh
:C )/NOPR
:C )
:C )*GET,_z1,ACTIVE,,KEYWORD,,MESHTOOL
:C )*IF,_z1,eq,1,THEN
:C )*create,ansuitmp
:C )*msg,note,
:C )Some functions of this menu cannot be used while the %/&
:C )MeshTool is active.
:C )*end
:C )/input,ansuitmp
:C )*ENDIF
:C )/GO
:K #(igesfail)
Fnc_KMESH_m
Fnc_LMESH_m
Sep_
-Areas-
Men_MapMshA
Fnc_AMESH_m
Fnc_AMESHtar
Sep_
-Volumes-
Men_MapMshV
```

```
Fnc_VMESH_m
Sep_
-Volume Sweep-
Fnc_EXTOPT_vswe
Fnc_VSWEEP_m
Sep_
-Tet Mesh From-
Fnc_FVMESH
:E END
:!
```

Go through the description line by line and refer back to the image of the menu that it makes. Notice how each command in the file is rendered in the menu.

Note that you can call existing ANSYS MAPDL menus and functions from your own custom menu. This allows you to make your own custom menu with your own collection and organization of commands. Companies often do this to provide occasional users with a reduced menu to help guide them through the analysis process.

10.3.3 UIDL Function Blocks

Once you define a Menu Block it is time to define the Function Blocks that are called by your menus. There are a lot of options available and it can become fairly complicated to create complex functions and dialogs. This is not a book on UIDL so we are just going to provide the basics. The actual ANSYS MAPDL menus are full of hundreds of examples that you can look at and learn from.

As with all blocks in UIDL, you first start with the Header. The commands are similar to those for Menus:

Command	Req.	Description	Example
:N Fnc_*String*	Yes	Defines Name of Block to be *String*	Fnc_/GSAVE
:S 0, 0, 0	Yes	Index Place Holder for Block. 0's must be in columns 9, 16 and 23, followed by commas	
:T CMD	Yes	Tells ANSYS the Block is a Function Block	:T Menu
:A *String*	No	Specifies that the name of the command as it will appear in the menu. Highly	:A Save Plot Ctrls

		recommended. If not used, Fnc_String will be used	
:D *String*	Yes	Provides the Heading for the Dialog Box. Placed in the title Bar	:D Save Plot Controls
:C *String*	No	Executes the ANSYS Command *String*. Prefix *string* with ")" to hide commands from log file and start with *:C)/nopr* to turn of echo to output window.	:C *del,_zx
:K *Keyword_Logic*	No	Filters the Block Based on Keywords. See Appendix A of Programming Manual	:K #((PREP7*SOLUTION)+ (CFD)
:P *Product_Logic*	No	Filters the Block Based Upon Product Codes See Appendix B of Programming Manual	:P (FLOTRAN)
:H *Hlp_string*	No	Internal name for the help for the dialog	:H Hlp_C_/GSAVE
:! *String*	No	Separator and Comments	:! End of Block
:E END	YES	Ends the Block	:E END

An example header is shown below with the block commands.

Once the header is defined, it is time to define your function. There are a lot of commands that give the user a large number of options on what they want their function to do. Many of them you will not use for a custom command, but it is good to know what they do so you will understand existing functions when you review them.

The way a function works is fairly simple. You define an APDL command you want to execute then you either specify the arguments, or prompt the user for arguments to fill in for that command. You can get those arguments through bringing up a picking dialog, an input dialog, or a file dialog. Everything is specified as a hierarchy:

- Command (Cmd_)
  - Field (Fld_)
    - Definition for Field (Def_, Typ_, Prm_, etc...)
  - ...

- Command (Cmd_)
  - Field (Fld_)
    - Definition for Field (Def_, Typ_, Prm_, etc...)
  - ...
- Command (Cmd_)
  - Field (Fld_)
    - Definition for Field (Def_, Typ_, Prm_, etc...)
  - ...
- ...
- :E END

The basic commands are:

Command	Description
Cmd_*string*	An APDL command to execute. String is the APDL command. When the function is executed, any parameters that are supplied will be issued as arguments to the command. You can have multiple commands in a block.
!	Comment
Cal_*Fnc_Block,FIELD, Oper,VALUE,CMDNUM*	Calls another function block. Must be used just before :E End command. If the FIELD,Oper,VALUE arguments are supplied an if test is done, and if it is true the call is made. CMDNUM refers to the data block that contains FIELD.
Cal_REFRESH	Forces a refresh of lowest active side menu
Fmt_H	Forces a narrow dialog
Inp_P	Defines a hidden or picking box function block
Inp_NoApply	Suppress the Apply button
K_LN	Sets keyword logic for next line
P_LN	Sets product code logic for next line
Pwr_*Flag*	Switches FLST and FITEM on and off for a field. Used with picking. *FLAG = 0* is the default and allows writing. 1 disables writing items. Used with *FENT and *FPIK commands

Rmk_	Forces a rebuild of a dialog after an Apply

The most important command in this table is Cmd_. It defines what APDL command or commands the function is executing. Any subsequent commands that come after one Cmd_ and before another or the end of the block, refer to that command.

You specify the arguments to build into the command with field commands:

Command	Description

Fld_*n*	Defines a field in a dialog box and specifies which Argument number in command specified in Cmd_ to which the contents of that field apply
	    Fld_0 is label/separator
	    Fld_1 is invalid
	    Fld_2 is first field that data goes in
	    Fld_n are subsequent fields

Dlm_*Char*	Delimits fields when building a command from Cmd_. The default of a comma is usually all that is needed. Use with a blank space after the underscore to build a space delimited string.
Def_*string*	Sets initial value for Field
K_FL_	Sets Keyword logic for current field
P_FL_	Sets Product logic for current field
Prm_*string*	Label or prompt for current field. Note that you can use string substitution here: %param%.

Key commands here are the Fld_, Def_ and Prm_ commands. They specify the field (argument) you are specifying, the default value, and the label for any prompt that might be created.

What is missing from the above commands is a way to specify how you want to prompt the user for the arguments. You do that with Typ_ commands. They define the type of widget or dialog box that will be presented to the user to gain input, or decorations (labels and separators) for the dialog box.

Command	Description

Typ_Int	Single Integer
Typ_Int2	Two Integers
Typ_Int3	Three Integers
Typ_Real	Single Real Number
Typ_Real2	Two Real Numbers
Typ_Real3	Three Real Numbers
Typ_Char	Character Input
Typ_Logi,falseval, trueval	On/Off Toggle Returns 0 or 1
Typ_File	File Selection Returns file,ext,dir
Typ_File_Inline	Text Box for File Name: Parses for OS to file,ext,dir
Typ_Color	Creates a Color Menu
Typ_Lis	Single Item Selection List
Typ_Lis_OptionB	Option Button List
Typ_Lis_RadioB	Radio Button List
Typ_Mlis	Multi-Selection Scrolling List
Typ_Idx	Side-by-Side Scrolling List
Typ_Lab	Label Text
Typ_Sep	Draws a Line Across Box to Separate
Typ_Def *string*	Creates a hidden field that is not shown in a dialog or anywhere else, and specifies the value for that field. Use this to automatically fill in a parameter. String can be a numerical value, a *GET command, a *PICK.

If you specify a Typ_Lis you have to define the values that you want listed and control on how users can pick things. You do this by using one of the following three commands:

Command	Description
Bnd_*min,max*	Sets Bounds on Type_MLis Boundaries define min and max number of choices. Must be real number separated by a comma Example: Bnd_1.0,5.0 Pick 1 to 5 values
Lis_*label,value*	Creates text to be listed in the various list controls. Value is the value that is provided to the command if the item is picked.
Lis_*READ,label*	Allows you to fill a list on the fly using values stored in the database. The values you can show are: ASSM defined assemblies CM defined components DOF degree-of-freedom set DV design variables ETAB element table items F force set FIT fitting functions MAT material numbers OBJ objective function OPTH list of paths PAR parameters PARX parameters not used as optimization Variables PATH path items REAL real constant numbers SV state variables TYPE element types

A very similar command is the IDX_*label1, label2, value* command. For Typ_Idx you can create an indexed list, sort of like a tree. It allows you to group items and then let the user pick from the group and see the options in that group. Label1 is the group, Label2 are the times in each group, and value is what is returned if the user picks it. See the example below to better understand how it works.

The best way to understand these commands is to see them in an example. Here is a simple one that saves the current graphics settings to a file. It prompts the user to specify a file with a file dialog (Typ_FILE)

```
:N Fnc_Pl_/GSAVE
:S    278,    181,     90
:T Cmd
:C )! Fnc_Pl_/GSAVE
:C )/NOPR
:C )*DEL,_zx
:C )*DIM,_zx,char,10,3,2
:C )/GO
:H Hlp_C_/GSAVE
:A Save Plot Ctrls
:D Save Plot Controls
:Fmt_H
Cmd_/GSAVE
Fld_2
   Prm_[/GSAVE] Save plot ctrls
   Typ_FILE
   Def_*PAR(_zx)
:E End
```

In the header we create a temporary character array called _zx that we can store the value that the user specifies in. That is just a nice thing to do in case you need it for something else. The actual command is /GSAVE which takes a file name as an argument, so Fld_2 is of Typ_File. The resulting dialog looks like this:

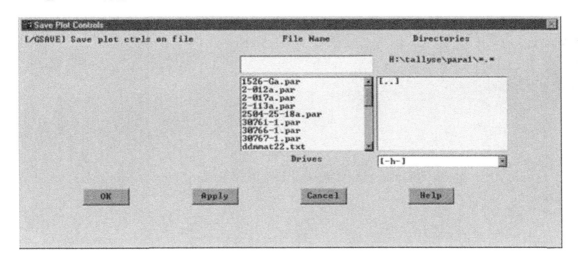

Figure 10.2: Save Plot Controls Dialog

10.3.4 A UIDL Example of Widgets

The following is a full UIDL definition of a menu, four functions, and a series of dialog boxes:

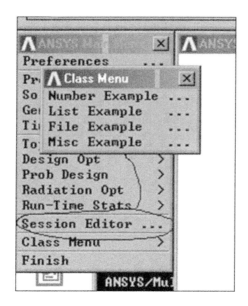

Figure 10.3: User Defined Menu

The first place to start is the menu definition. Create a menu that calls four functions: one for each type of dialog:

```
:!-----------------------
:N Men_ClassAddon
:S      0,      0,      0
:T Menu
:A Class Menu
:D Class Addon Menu
Fnc_numberExp
Fnc_lisExp
Fnc_fileExp
Fnc_miscExp
:E END
```

To create the dialog for showing the options for prompting for numbers, use this definition:

```
:!-----------------------------
:N Fnc_numberExp
:S      0,      0,      0
:T CMD
:A Number Example
:D Example Number Dialog Widgets
Fmt_H
Cmd_/Com
 Fld_0
  Typ_Lab
  Prm_Sample Number Data...
```

```
Fld_0
 Typ_Sep
Fld_0
 Typ_Lab
 Prm_Integers:
Fld_2
 Typ_Int
 Prm_Single Integer
Fld_3
 Typ_Int2
 Prm_Two Integers
Fld_4
 Typ_Int3
 Prm_Three Integers
Fld_0
 Typ_Sep
Fld_0
 Prm_Float Numbers:
Fld_4
 Typ_Real
 Prm_Single Float
Fld_5
 Typ_Real2
 Prm_Two Floats
Fld_5
 Typ_Real3
 Prm_Three Floats
:E END
```

This is fairly simple. Note how the headings for each section, and the separators, use Fld_0 to tell the program that they are not actual parameters that will get fed to any commands. Here is what the dialog looks like:

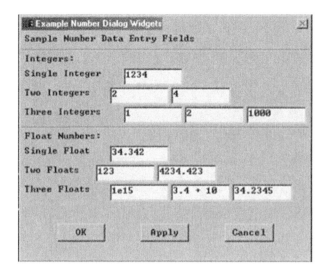

Figure 10.4: Example Number Dialog Widget

Lists can be very useful because they save the user a lot of time when it comes to entering data, and constricts their choices to only valid ones. What makes them different is that you have to define the choices.

We will break the granule up into chunks to look at each type of list, but remember they need to be put into one granule. The resulting dialog will look like this:

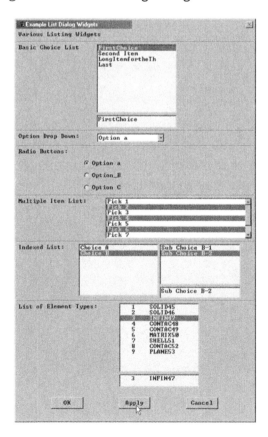

Figure 10.5: Example List Widgets

The place to start is with the header:

```
:!---------
:N Fnc_lisExp
:S       0,       0,       0
:T CMD
:A List Example
:D Example List Dialog Widgets
:C)/nopr
:C)/prep7
:C)et,1,45
:C)rp9,1,1
:C)/go
Fmt_H
Cmd_/Com
  Fld_0
    Typ_Lab
    Prm_Various Listing Widgets
```

There is nothing special in the header except for the APDL code to make nine element types. This is done so that when we use LIS_*READ we have something in the database to read. If you use this code for your own menu, remember to delete that part.

A simple list is the first list we will add to the widget.

```
Fld_0
  Typ_Sep
  Fld_2
  Typ_Lis
    Lis_FirstChoice,1
    Lis_Second Item,2
    Lis_LongItemfortheThirdPick,3
    Lis_Last,100
    Prm_Basic Choice List
```

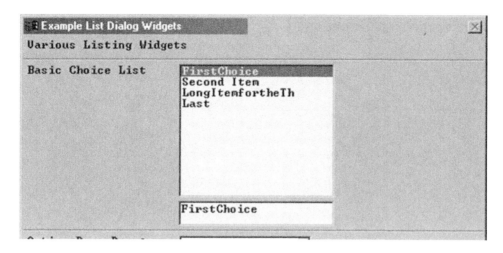

Figure 10.6: Choice Widget

Note how we have called this field 2 (Fld_2) and given it four choices with values of 1,2,3,100.

You have two choices for asking the user a multiple choice question. One is a drop down and the other is a radio button. The radio buttons are preferred for up to about four choices, after that, use the drop down. For fields 4 and 5:

```
Fld_0
  Typ_Sep
 Fld_3
  Typ_Lis_OptionB
  Lis_Option a,opta,1
  Lis_Option_B,Second Choice,2
  Lis_Option C,3
Prm_Option Drop Down:
Fld_0
  Typ_Sep
Fld_4
 Typ_lis_RadioB
 Lis_Option a,opta,1
 Lis_Option_B,Second Choice,2
 Lis_Option C,3
Prm_Radio Buttons:
```

It produces the following two widgets:

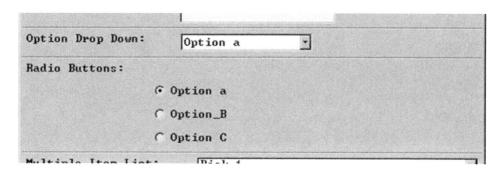

Figure 10.7: Drop Down and Radio Button Widgets

When you need to have a user pick more than one option, you use a Multi List with Typ_MLIS:

```
Fld_0
  Typ_Sep
  Fld_5
  Typ_MLis
  Bnd_3.0,3.0
   Lis_Pick 1,A
   Lis_Pick 2,B
   Lis_Pick 3,C
   Lis_Pick 4,D
   Lis_Pick 5,E
   Lis_Pick 6,F
   Lis_Pick 7,G
   Lis_Pick 8,H
   Lis_Pick 9,I
  Prm_Multiple Item List:
```

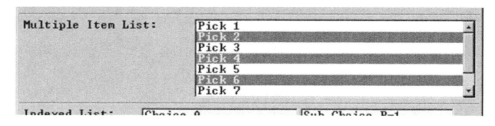

Figure 10.8: Multiple Picking Widget

The next type of list is the most complicated, the Indexed List. It is a way to group choices so you are not presenting so many to the user. It uses the Typ_Idx and Idx_ commands. You list every choice option, specifying a group label and the actual label. Then the user is presented with the list of groups, once they pick that group they get a list of all the choices within the group:

```
Fld_0
  Typ_Sep
```

```
Fld_6
 Typ_Idx
  Idx_Choice A    ,Sub Choice A-1,  1
  Idx_Choice A    ,Sub Choice A-2,  2
  Idx_Choice A    ,Sub Choice A-3,  3
  Idx_Choice B    ,Sub Choice B-1,  4
  Idx_Choice B    ,Sub Choice B-2,  5
 Prm_Indexed List:
```

The last list is one of the more useful ones, generating a list of items from the database with Lis_*READ. In our example we will be listing all the element types in the database. Also note that since this is the last widget type, we will close everything out with a :END.

```
Fld_0
   Typ_Sep
  Fld_7
   Typ_Lis
    Lis_*Read,TYPE
   Prm_List of Element Types:
:E END
```

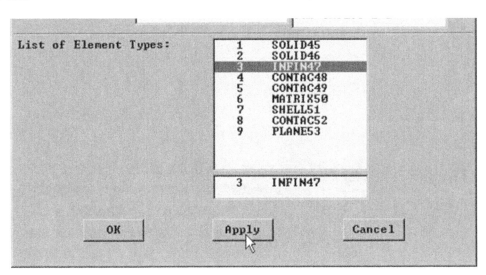

Figure 10.9: Database Items List Widget

Moving on to the next dialog, we will add the function to show the file dialog. You can get files in one of two ways. The first is to use the built in file picker and the other is to simply ask for the file name as a text string. It is almost always better to use the file picker.

```
:!---------------------------------------------
:N Fnc_fileExp
:S     0,     0,     0
:T CMD
```

```
:A File Example
:D Example File Dialog Widgets
Fmt_H
Cmd_/Com
 Fld_0
  File Name and Selection Widgets
 Fld_0
  Typ_Sep
 Fld_2
  Typ_File
  Prm_Use Built In File Picker
 Fld_0
  Typ_Sep
 Fld_3
  Typ_File_Inline
  Prm_Just ask for a long string
:E END
```

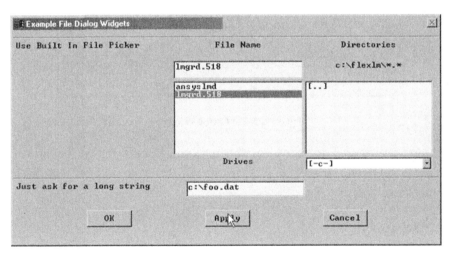

Figure 10.10: File Dialog Widget

There are a few remaining options available that are shown in the last dialog. The check box and character string are the most useful.

```
:!---------------------------------------------
:N Fnc_miscExp
:S      0,      0,      0
:T CMD
:A Misc Example
:D Example Misc. Dialog Widgets
Fmt_H
Cmd_/Com
 Fld_0
  Prm_Various Different Dialog Widgets
```

```
Fld_2
 Typ_Char
 Prm_Character String:
Fld_3
 Typ Logi,No Choice, Yes Choice
 Prm_Logic Choice
Fld_4
 Typ_Color
 Prm_Color Choices
:E END
```

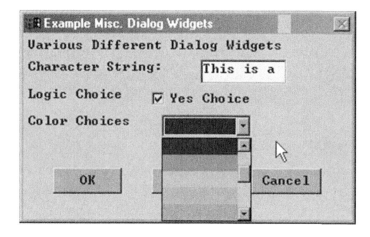

Figure 10.11: Other Widgets

It is a good idea to try and get some of these example widgets to work before you try customizing your own user interface. A bit tricky at first, once you get used to it the whole process can be very useful.

10.3.5 UIDL Pick Function

It is very common to need the user to pick entities in the graphics window to provide values for a parameter in a command. Fortunately this is fairly easy to do using the :T Cmd_P type with :Inp_P. The commands are:

Command	Description
Typ_Entity	Specifies the Entity Type to be Picked Valid Entity values are: NODE, ELEM, KEYP, LINE, AREA, VOLU, TRAC
Typ_Resu	Pick Results from a Solution
Typ_XYZ	Obtain Coordinates of a Point

`Typ_XYZ_SCREEN`	Obtain the coordinates of a point in the screen units
`Typ_XYZ_WP`	Gets coordinates of a point in the working plain coordinate system

In addition to these commands, there is the ability to define a "rubber band" to use in the picking. Sort of a fence. You can also use it to create electric circuits. Specify Rub_N where N is:

Table 10.1: Picking Options

For 2D Picking on Working Plane		3D Picking on WP & Z Dimension	
1	Lines	101	Polyhedron
2	Rectangle (Corner - Opposite Corner)	102	Block
3	Circle (Center - Radius)	103	Cylinder-solid
4	Annulus (Center - R1 & R2)	104	Cylinder-hollow
5	Partial Annulus	105	Partial Cylinder
6	Rectangle (Center - Corner)	106	Block (Center - Corner)
7	Circle (On Circle - On Circle)	107	Cylinder-solid (On Circle - On Circle)
8	Rectangle (Center - Edge)	109	Cone
13	3 Equal-sided Polygon	113	3 Equal-sided Polyhedron
14	4 Equal-sided Polygon	114	4 Equal-sided Polyhedron
15	5 Equal-sided Polygon	115	5 Equal-sided Polyhedron
16	6 Equal-sided Polygon	116	6 Equal-sided Polyhedron
17	7 Equal-sided Polygon	117	7 Equal-sided Polyhedron
18	8 Equal-sided Polygon	118	8 Equal-sided Polyhedron
For 3D Picking Between Keypoints		**Electrical Circuits (3 Points to Create)**	
51	Straight Lines	201	Inductor
52	Lines In Active Csys	202	Capacitor
53	Area In Active Csys	203	Resistor
54	Area With Straight Lines	204	Circuit 1
		205	Circuit 2
		206	Circuit 3
		207	Circuit 4

To illustrate how the command is used, the following example does a keypoint list command:

```
:N Fnc_pickExp
:S    0,    0,    0
:T Cmd_P
:A Pick Example
:D Pick Example: KP List
:Inp_P
   Cmd_KLIST
```

```
        Fld_2
          Typ_Keyp
          Prm_[KLIST] Pick Keyoints
          Rub_53
          Min_1
          Cnt_s
    :E End
```

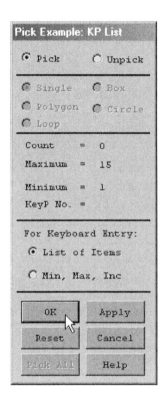

Table 10.2: Sample Picking Dialog

10.3.6 Hidden Function Blocks

You may want to create a command in the menu that does not actually bring up a dialog box or do picking. This is called a hidden function and it just executes whatever APDL commands you put in as :C lines. It is a bit of a trick in that you actually specify a picking dialog but tell the program not to use it with Inp_P and Cmd_)! As an example, here is a command that compresses all the numbers in your model:

```
:N Fnc_hidExp
:S     0,     0,     0
:T Cmd
:A Hidden Compress All
:C)! Fnc_hidExp
:C)/go
:C)/prep7
:C)numcmp,all
```

```
    Inp_P
    Cmd_)!
:E END
```

It is type Cmd but for the command to execute, you tell it)! which means do not do anything.

10.4   UIDL Suggestions and Recommendations

In order to make sure your interface does not confuse or surprise users, and to make it easier to follow what you did in the future, the following recommendations should be followed:

— ANSYS command names in labels must be all uppercase and enclosed in brackets
— Use the same case for field names as in the ANSYS Manual
— Separate Unrelated Items in a Dialog with the Typ_Sep command
— Use blanks to separate between words. Don't use characters like –, + or *
— When you break a Typ_Lab into multiple lines, use a – at the end and beginning of each line to show that it was "cut"
— Capitalize Your Dialog and Menu Headings
— Make dialog and menu headings descriptive but short
— Avoid using a scroll bar in a dialog, try to keep lists short

Some things you should be very careful about are:

— Never try and use a pick and a dialog function together. It is not robust
— Do not place verbose documentation in the UIDL file. It slows down the Menus and can result in a syntax error that is hard to track down
— If you have an error, lines may be deleted from your file. Never test with your source file, always copy it to a GRN file.
— For better readability, separate each function block with a :! Line :!----------------------------- Is even better
— Do not mix K_ and P_ commands unless you only use them once each
— Use Rmk_ to rebuild dialogs that change after an apply
— A line in a control file cannot be more than 80 characters

There is also a handy debugging trick to see when a function is called. Add the line :C)!Fnc_funcname to the header. In ANSYS MAPDL, type KEYW,QALOGKEY,1 and the a string will be written to output whenever the function is called.

Chapter 11:   Building Custom GUI's with Tcl/Tk

11.1 Tcl/TK and its History

The Tcl/Tk (Tool Command Language/Tool Kit) was developed in 1989 at the University of California, Berkeley by John Ousterhout. There are two separate products - Tcl is a versatile scripting language and Tk is a graphical interface development tool. They were initially developed to interface with the X11 windowing system and are now integrated into ANSYS MAPDL as the graphical user interface that is used when the program is run interactively.

ANSYS MAPDL adopted Tcl/TK as an interface to replace the proprietary GUI that was developed internally based on XWindows. Tcl/TK allowed the development team the ability to have a cross platform GUI that sits on top of the program, providing portability and flexibility at a very low cost. As the ANSYS Workbench line of products have grown to replace the ANSYS MAPDL GUI as the way most users work interactively, the Tcl/TK interface has not been updated. But it still works well and still serves its purpose, even if it is looking a bit dated.

11.2 Advantages of Tcl/Tk

There are four reasons that Tcl/Tk is a superior option and they are Price, Facility, Flexibility, and Compatibility. 1) Price – Tcl/Tk is available as a *free* download. 2) Facilities – Tcl/Tk is relatively easy to learn compared to other software languages such as Visual C++ and Visual Fortran. Tcl/Tk is also interpretive, so one can immediately see effects of the program without recompiling code. 3) There is flexibility – it is already imbedded in numerous tools which allow you to create and organize entry boxes, canvases, etc. Tools and commands may be created either in the programming environment, or by editing source code to create a custom interpreter. 4) Compatibility – it is cross platform compatible, e.g. scripts written in Windows will also run on Linux and Mac OS x, provided that Tcl/Tk is installed on each.

There are additional reasons to use Tcl/Tk in ANSYS MAPDL. One big one is that the Tkl/TK interpreter has been compiled into the program, giving a programmer direct access through Tcl/TK. This opens a lot of doors to some sophisticated interaction. The most common reason for using Tcl/TK is that it provides an easy way to create a GUI on top of ANSYS MAPDL for a custom tool, rather than creating a separate program that has to talk through files to ANSYS MAPDL.

The integration also makes it easy to integrate your own Tcl/TK scripts and GUI widgets into the ANSYS MAPDL menu, making interaction very easy for your users. And lastly, because it is built into the program, you do not have to worry about installing and maintaining a third party library or tool set on every users machine – if they have ANSYS MAPDL, they have Tcl/TK.

11.3 The Pros and Cons of Using Tcl/Tk to Customize

Before anyone digs into Tcl/Tk it should be stated that the GUI for ANSYS Mechanical APDL is in maintenance mode. This is not an interface that will be improved or worked on in the future, and it is also an interface that fewer and fewer users even know how to use. Anything you create in Tcl/Tk will be a bit unique and will be a dead end.

The positives of Tcl/Tk are the advantages listed above. The integration with ANSYS Mechanical APDL is very tight, and there are no real limits on what you can do with this tool.

The newer tools from ANSYS, Inc., as of this writing, are mostly python based which has even more power and capability than Tcl/Tk. Before considering the use of Tcl/Tk you should try that path first.

11.4 Tcl/Tk Syntax

Tcl/Tk files for ANSYS are located in C:\Program Files\Ansys Inc\v(your version of ANSYS here)\ ANSYS\gui\scripts. Tcl/Tk files have the extension *.eui. If you look in some of those files you can get a feel for the syntax. It is not too far removed from other scripting languages and is very readable.

```
# Element Type ID's
if [info exists defETypes] (
    set defElemTypes [join [join $defETypes]]
) else (
    set defElemTypes 0
)

if ($elemFound != 0) (

    # Nodal Components
    set numComponents [ans_getvalue COMP,,NCOMP]
    for (set i 0) ($i <= $numComponents) (incr i) (
        set nameComponent($i) [ans_getvalue COMP,$i,NAME]
        set typeComponent($i) [ans_getvalue COMP,$nameComponent($i),TYPE]
        if ($typeComponent($i) == 1) (
            lappend nodeComponents $nameComponent($i)
        )
    )
    if [info exists nodeComponents] (
        variable NodalComponents [join [join $nodeComponents]]
    ) else (
        variable NodalComponents 0
    )

    # Material ID's
    set defMaterials [list]
    set defMaterialList [ans_getlist MAT]
    foreach (name id) $defMaterialList (
        lappend defMaterials [string trim $id]
    )
    if ([string match "()" $defMaterials]) (
```

Table 11.1: Code from contactWizard.eui

11.5 Tcl/Tk Resources

Some of the resource for the Tcl/Tk are:

- Books
    - Tcl and the Tk ToolKit, by John Ousterhout
    - *Effective Tcl/Tk Programming*, by Mark Harrison and Michael McLennan
- Links
    - Tcl Developer Exchange: http://www.tcl.tk/
    - Tcl/Tk Information Page: http://www.tcl.tk/about/
    - Various The Focus articles written by PADT that can be found by searching on "Tcl/TK" at http://www.padtinc.com/blog
- Downloads
    - Most everything you need for Tcl/Tk can be found at http://www.tcl.tk

11.6 Using Tcl/Tk with ANSYS Mechanical APDL

The use of Tcl/Tk to customize the interface in ANSYS Mechanical APDL really opens up the door to any sophisticated user interface changes you want to do, including the replacement of the full interface with your own.

Here are some examples of user interfaces built by ANSYS, Inc. for Mechanical APDL that used Tcl/TK:

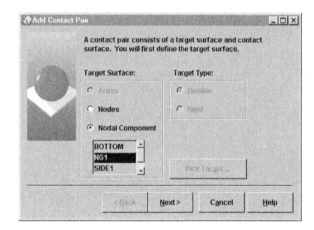
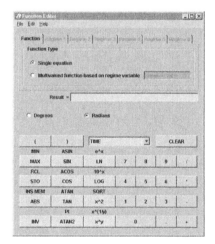

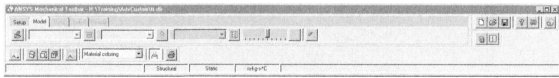

Table 11.2: Tcl/Tk Examples in ANSYS MAPDL

The key to effectively using Tcl/Tk for a custom interface is to remember that ANSYS Mechanical APDL is command based, and instead of using a script or UIDL to build a command and send it, you use Tcl/Tk. There are tools provided to allow you to get and put information from and to the database as well. There really are few limits on what you can do with Tcl/Tk in ANSYS MAPDL.

To run a Tcl/Tk script that is in a file you have three options:

- ~tcl, source filename
  - o This tells APDL to run a non-GUI (tcl) script.
- ~tk, source filename
  - o Run a Tcl/Tk script that does GUI things
- ~eui, source filename
  - o Run a Tcl/Tk script that includes higher level object oriented libraries including [incr Tcl] and [incr Tk] as well as some ANSYS specific Tcl/Tk functions.

To play it safe, you are always better using ~eui.

11.7 A Quick Example: Hello World!

As with any programming language, you should always start with Hello World!

```
destroy .hello
set t [toplevel .hello]
wm title $t "Sample Hello Program"
label $t.msg -text "Greetings and Salutations from Tcl/Tk!"
frame $t.frame
button $t.frame.b1 -text "Goodbye!" -width 10 -command {
    set answer [tk_messageBox -icon question \
            -message "Are you sure?" -type okcancel]
    if {$answer == "ok"} {destroy .hello}
}
pack $t.frame.b1 $t.msg  $t.frame
```

Place this code into a text file called helloworld.tcl then within Mechanical APDL type in the command:

```
~tk, source helloworld.tcl
```

You will get:

Table 11.3: Hello World Output

Take a good look at this code. If the code makes some sense, then you are good. If it does not, you should really ask yourself if you need to create a custom user interface on a user interface (ANSYS Mechanical APDL) that is in maintenance mode. Learning a legacy programming language can be a bit frustrating. Many people program at the ANSYS Mechanical level or use python to create interfaces that then run ANSYS Mechanical APDL in batch mode.

11.8 Special Add In Commands for Working with ANSYS Mechanical APDL

What makes Tcl/Tk so useful is that it is integrated into the program. So you can send data back and forth from your script, and you can execute ANSYS commands. The important commands are shown here with example. They are pretty self-explanatory:

```
ans_getvalue ansGetComand
set ansRev [ans_getvalue active,,rev]
set nxval [ans_getvalue node,1,loc,x]


ans_getvector Arrayname
  set aa [ans_getvector tt]
  puts $aa


ans_sendcommand command
  set a 14
  set b 15
  ans_sendcommand k,$a,2,3,0
  ans_sendcommand k,$b,3,3,0
  ans_sendcommand l,$a,$b


ans_writeout string
  ans_writeour $myMessage
```

11.9 A More ANSYS Oriented Tcl/Tk Example

In this example we actually communicate to and from ANSYS Mechanical APDL:

```
destroy .noder
set t [toplevel .noder]
set _nx 0
set _ny 0

label $t.l -text "Create Node at Specified X and Y Value"
label $t.lx -text "X: "
label $t.ly -text "Y: "
entry $t.e_nx -textvariable _nx -bg white
entry $t.e_ny -textvariable _ny -bg white
button $t.btnOK -text OK -bg grey -command {
```

```
    ans_sendcommand "*set, _nx, $_nx"
    ans_sendcommand "*set, _ny, $_ny"
    ans_sendcommand "*set,_BUTTON,2"
    ans_sendcommand "n,,_nx,_ny"
    destroy $t
}
grid config $t.l   -row 1 -column 1 -columnspan 2
grid config $t.lx  -row 2 -column 1 -sticky e
grid config $t.ly -row 3 -column 1 -sticky e
grid config $t.e_nx -row 2 -column 2 -sticky w
grid config $t.e_ny -row 3 -column 2 -sticky w
grid config $t.btnOK -row 4 -column 1 -columnspan 2 -pady 5
```

It prompts the user for an X and Y value then creates a node at that value.

11.10 Learning More

If you are serious about using Tcl/Tk with ANSYS Mechanical APDL you will need additional information.   A   copy   of   PADT's   original   Tcl/Tk   course   can   be   found   on   our   blog: www.padtinc.com/blog. Just search for tcl/tk.

Chapter 12:   APDL Math

12.1   Introduction to APDL Math

You have always been able to get at the underlying linear algebra inside the Mechanical APDL solver through a large collection of FOTRAN routines. Over the years this has been OK but other competitive software offered easier access to vectors, matrices, and solvers and let users do their own thing without having to compile. APDL Math was introduced over several versions as an answer to this need, giving full and complete access to what is going on inside, and allowing users to import, export, and manipulate vectors and matrices easily and quickly through the powerful APDL language.

APDL MATH is an extension to the APDL command language that drives Mechanical APDL. Although it runs in a different workspace (chunk of memory in the ANSYS database) it talks to standard APDL by importing and exporting APDL arrays (vectors or matrices). It consists of 20 commands that can be executed at the /SOLU level at any time. All of the commands start with a * character and look and act like standard APDL commands.

APDL Math is a tool for users to do two things: 1) get access to view, export, or modify matrices and vectors created by the solver, and 2) to control, import, or modify matrices and vectors then solve them. The solvers include same solvers used in normal ANSYS Mechanical APDL solutions including the distributed solvers.

The most common use is the exporting of a matrix from ANSYS for use in some other program, usually Matlab. The other is working with sub-structure matrices for inclusion in large system models that use component mode synthesis. Some users create and solve their own matrix systems with this tool.

This chapter is a very quick overview to give the reader an idea of how APDL Math works and what they can do with it. Please see ANSYS Help for details and examples.

12.2   APDL Math Commands

The commands for APDL Math are divided into four groups: creating and deleting, manipulating, solving, and outputting. Note that names are assigned to matrices and vectors and then used in commands as identifiers.

Commands to create and delete matrices and vectors

*DMAT: Creates a dense matrix

*SMAT: Creates a sparse matrix

> These commands can be used in a variety of ways to create a matrix from an existing matrix, from a file, or as an empty matrix. Use *DMAT for dense matrices

and *SMAT for sparse. The matrix can be made of double precision, complex double precision, or integer numbers. It can also be used to resize a matrix and additional options on the command allow the user to request that the matrix be transposed as it is created or that it is a subset of an existing matrix. *SMAT also allows for the creation of a diagonal only matrix.

The following ANSYS matrix files can be read and their contents stored in an APDL Math matrix: FULL, MODE, CMS, TCMS, RST, SUB, and RFRQ.

In addition, the command can read other non ANSYS formats including: Harwell-Boeing (HBMAT), Matrix Market (MMF), and NASTRAN DMIG.

It also reads its own internal MAT format.

*VEC: Creates a vector

This command is just like *DMAT and *SMAT except it only does a vector. The same options and file formats are available.

*FREE: Deletes a matrix or a solver object and frees its memory allocation.

This cleans up the matrix and frees the memory. Since the amount of memory used is huge, it is always a good idea to *FREE a matrix when you don't need it any longer. *FREE, all clears all the matrices as does a /CLEAR command.

Commands to manipulate matrices

This collection of commands is the heart of the tools used to do matrix math and manipulation. They are all pretty self-explanatory and are the most common operations found in any matrix too. All operations work with real and imaginary matrices and work with matrix names.

*AXPY: Performs the matrix operation M2= v*M1 + w*M2

*COMP: Compresses the columns of a matrix using a specified algorithm

*COMP support Singular Value Decomposition (default), Modified Gram-Schmidt, or a sparse matrix method that removes values below a threshold value. The matrix is resized to the size of the compressed matrix.

*DOT: Computes the dot (or inner) product of two vectors

*FFT: Computes the fast Fourier transformation of the specified matrix or vector

This provides a full Fast Fourier transformation, both forwards and backwards.

*INIT: Initializes a vector or dense matrix

> This allows the user to fill a vector with values rather than reading them in or calculating them. It supports: zeros, a constant, random values, constants on a diagonal, constants on an anti-diagonal, complex conjugate values, and a filtering method.

*MERGE: Merges two dense matrices or vectors into one

*MULT: Performs the matrix multiplication M3 = M1(T1)*M2(T2)

> This command helps out by having a "transpose" key so you don't have to transpose a matrix before you multiply it. The first or second matrix can be transposed. *MULT does not work on two sparse matrices, only dens*sparse, sparse*dens, or dense*dense. The result is always dense.

*NRM: Computes the norm of the specified vector or matrix

> *NRM supports three methods to compute a norm: Euclidian or SRSS, absolute sum (vectors only), or Maximum. You can also normalize a vector to 1 with this command.

*REMOVE: Suppresses rows or columns of a dense matrix or a vector

Commands to perform solutions

Once you have the matrices and vectors you want, you can solve them inside ANSYS using the powerful solvers there. You set up the solve with *LSENGINE and *LSFACTOR and then use the other commands to actually execute the solve. The ANSYS distributed solvers are available with these commands. These commands have a lot of options, beyond the scope of this chapter. Please see the online help or details.

*LSENGINE	Creates a linear solver engine
*LSFACTOR	Performs the numerical factorization of a linear solver system
*LSBAC	Performs the solve of a factorized linear system
*ITENGINE	Performs a solution using an iterative solver
*EIGEN	Performs a modal solution with unsymmetric or damping matrices

Commands to output matrices

Once you have the matrix or vector you want, you can output them to a file or to APDL. You can also print them in a readable format.

`*EXPORT`: Exports a matrix to a file in the specified format

> This is the opposite of *SMAT and *DMAT. It writes matrices and vectors to various file formats as well as to an APDL array parameter. External format that are supported include: Matrix Market (MMF), Harwell-Boeing (HBMAT), and NASTRAN DMIG. A PostScript options shows a graphical representation of a sparse matrix as dots.

`*PRINT`: Prints the matrix values to a file

12.3 Workshop 12: APDL Math Example

In this workshop we will build a simple beam model and then use APDL Math to extract, modify, write, and solve various matrices. The beam model is 10 nodes with six DOF's per node, so the stiffness matrix is 60 x 60.

1: Make sure that bb1.mac is in your working directory. It can be found the in 'inputs and demos' folder. It is a simple macro that creates a 10 element beam model:

```
finish                        mptemp,1,0
/clear                        MPDATA,EX,1,1,1e6
/file,bb1                     MPDATA,PRXY,1,1,.23
/PREP7                        MPDATA,DENS,1,1,.003
K,1,0,0,0,                    SECTYPE,1, BEAM, RECT, , 0
K,2,0,0,10,                   SECOFFSET, CENT
LSTR,1,2                      SECDATA,.125,.125
lplot                         finish
ET,1,BEAM188                  /solu
esize,1                       save
lmesh,all                     solve
/pnum,node,1                  FINISH
eplot                         /POST1
d,1,all                       plnsol,u,sum
f,2,fx,100                    pldisp,2
```

2: Run the macro to create a model and some matrices to work with by typing bb1 on the command line. Look in the working directory and you should see the files created in the run including the FULL file. Read in the stiffness matrix with the *SMAT command, save it to a text file, and view it:

```
*SMAT,K1,D,IMPORT,FULL,bb1.full,STIFF
*print,K1,k1.txt
*list,k1.txt
```

That should produce this output:

```
*LIST   Command                                                    ✕

File

 LISTING OF THE DATA ON FILE k1.txt

K1:
[ 1,  1]: 2.139e+003 [ 1,  7]:-1.070e+003 [ 1,11]: 5.349e+002
[ 2,  2]: 2.139e+003 [ 2,  8]:-1.070e+003 [ 2,10]:-5.349e+002
[ 3,  3]: 3.125e+004 [ 3,  9]:-1.562e+004
[ 4,  4]: 5.756e+002 [ 4,  8]: 5.349e+002 [ 4,10]: 2.471e+002
[ 5,  5]: 5.756e+002 [ 5,  7]:-5.349e+002 [ 5,11]: 2.471e+002
[ 6,  6]: 2.831e+001 [ 6,12]:-1.416e+001
[ 7,  7]: 2.139e+003 [ 7,13]:-1.070e+003 [ 7,17]: 5.349e+002
[ 8,  8]: 2.139e+003 [ 8,14]:-1.070e+003 [ 8,16]:-5.349e+002
[ 9,  9]: 3.125e+004 [ 9,15]:-1.562e+004
[10,10]: 5.756e+002 [10,14]: 5.349e+002 [10,16]: 2.471e+002
[11,11]: 5.756e+002 [11,13]:-5.349e+002 [11,17]: 2.471e+002
[12,12]: 2.831e+001 [12,18]:-1.416e+001
```

3: Not very useful, so let's try exporting it to PostScript. Execute this command:

```
*export,K1,PS,k1.ps,COLOR
```

Which should produce this image:

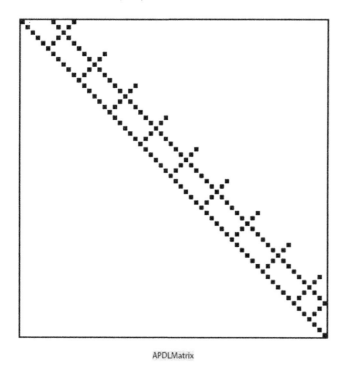

APDLMatrix

4: Save it to Harwell-Boeing, and Matrix Market format:

```
*export,K1,HBMAT, k1.hbmat, ascii
*export,K1,MMF, k1.mmf
```

Take a look at these two files in a text editor and make sure you understand what is happening.

5: Next we want to solve the model as a model problem:

```
finish
/filename,bb2
/solu
antype,2
MXPAND,5, , ,0
MODOPT,LANB,5,0,0, ,OFF
solve
```

6: To show off extraction and matrix multiplication, we will verify that the Eigenmodes are orthogonal. To do this we need the mass matrix and the mode shapes. Then we multiply them together, with the transpose, and should get the unity matrix:

(Phi)T*M*Phi where phi is the eigenmodes and (Phi)T is the transpose of Phi.

```
*SMAT,MM1,D,IMPORT,FULL,bb2.full,MASS
*SMAT,BCS1,D,IMPORT,FULL,bb2.full,NOD2BCS

*DMAT,Phi,D,IMPORT,MODE,bb2.mode
*MULT,BCS1,,Phi,,BCSPhi
*MULT,MM1,,BCSPhi,,APhi
*MULT,BCSPhi,TRANS,APhi,,mtrx1

*PRINT,mtrx1,mtrx1.txt
*list,mtrx1.txt
```

End of Workshop

Chapter 13:   Using APDL in ANSYS Mechanical

13.1 Introduction

ANSYS Mechanical is an incredibly powerful tool. It gives users access to considerable capability in a modern, intuitive, easy to user interface. This power is delivered by the fact that ANSYS Mechanical is actually a tool that builds commands for ANSYS Mechanical APDL. And those commands are written in APDL.

As time has passed, the capabilities of the program have grown and most of what users want can be found in ANSYS Mechanical. But sometimes you need features in ANSYS Mechanical APDL that are not found in ANSYS Mechanical, but you don't want to leave the ANSYS Mechanical interface. In these cases, the developers at ANSYS have offered us a great solution.

Users can add their own APDL scripts to an ANSYS Mechanical model as a code snippet. These snippets are added directly to the branches in your model tree, that way they are always there and available in your model. This gives users access to the full depth and breadth of capabilities without having to have them supported in ANSYS Mechanical.

13.2 Command Objects

ANSYS Mechanical takes an object oriented approach to describing a model. Each step in the modeling process is represented as a branch on the model tree. When the user asks for a solve, this tree is traversed and APDL commands are used to describe the model. These commands can be added to with a simple object, simply called a command object.

The object in the tree has an icon with a text document and a red C on it. It also has the words "Commands (APDL)" to describe it. Command objects can contain text commands for a variety of programs supported by ANSYS Mechanical, but for this book we will only talk about APDL.

Command objects are not perfect. Remember they get added to the input file for the solver. So if you add or delete entities in the ANSYS Mechanical APDL solve session, those changes do not make their way back to ANSYS Mechanical. Another shortcoming is that the input file does not contain any geometry, so you can't really use APDL to work with geometry.

The biggest drawback to Command Objects is that they are not interactive. You can't type in a command like you can in ANSYS Mechanical APDL and see what happens. This can be frustrating and we recommend that you actually save your APDL input file from ANSYS Mechanical and work with it in ANSYS Mechanical APDL, reading it in up to where your command object is. The interactively work on your command object, get it right, then include it in your ANSYS Mechanical model.

13.3   Adding APDL Command Objects

To add a command object, click on the Commands Icon or by using the Right Mouse Button (RMB) and choosing Insert > Commands:

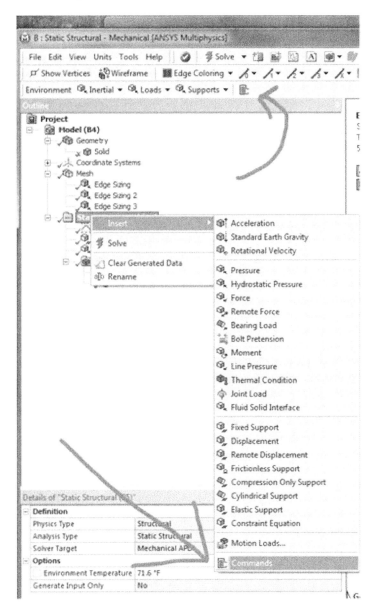

Figure 13.1: Inserting Command Objects

The commands you enter into the object are inserted in to the solver input file in the order you insert them. So if you want, you could put three in a row, where each one does something specific.

Once an object is in the tree, you can click on it and a tab becomes available in the user interface called "Commands." You can view and edit your APDL code here.

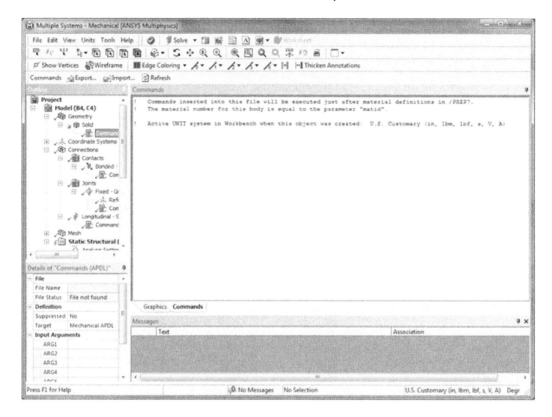

Figure 13.2: Commands Tab

You can of course type your commands in, or paste them from a text editor. Or, if you have a text file that you want to use and don't want to call it, you can specify the file name in the Details for the command object by using the Right Mouse Button on the command object and choosing "Import." You can also export the contents of the Commands tab or refresh if you have changed a file you imported earlier. This is important. If you change the file, it will not get updated in your model automatically. You will have to refresh the object manually.

The following figure shows the menu choices, what the resulting file name looks like in the details view, and how it looks in the tree:

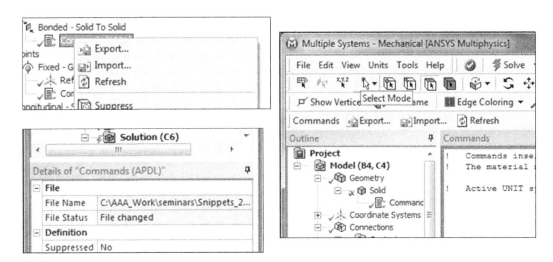

Figure 13.3: Assigning a File to a Command Object

There are three types of Command Objects: Items, Prep, and Post. They type determines where in the tree you insert the object and also where in the ANSYS Mechanical APDL input file the objects are put.

Item Command Objects are attached to an item in the tree and contain APDL that modifies only that item. If you look at the Command tab, and item ID is assigned for you to use in your APDL. These commands are executed in the /PREP7 module right after the item they refer to is defined.

Prep Command Objects are general commands that are executed in the /SOLVE module. They are inserted right before the solve command in the file.

Post Command Objects are, as the name implies, post processing commands that are executed in /POST1 right after the solve is finished.

The following figure shows some typical examples for a model:

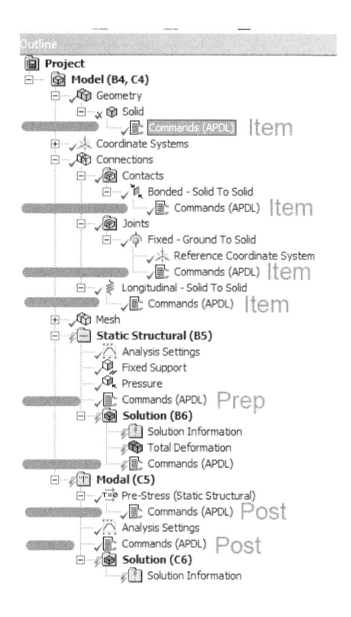

Figure 13.4: Examples of where Command Objects can be Inserted

Note: Although the command objects will specify a module, you can use APDL to go to a different module. Say go from /SOLU to /PREP7, you need a /SOLU at the end of your command object to make sure you return to the right module, otherwise the commands in the input file may not work.

The following table summarizes what you should know about Command Snippets based on where they go in the model tree. Note the ID column especially.

Type	Tree Object	Inserted in APDL File	ID
ITEM	Body	After material for that body is defined	MATID
	Contact Pair	After contact is defined	TID, CID for Type, Real and Mat
	Joint	After the joint definition	_JID
	Spring	After spring definition	_SID.
PREP	Environment	Right Before the Solve Command	
POST	Solution	Right after the /POST1 command	
	Pre-Stress	Before first solve in Pre-stress modal	

Table 13.1: Types of Command Objects

One of the most common requests for command objects are defining material properties that are not supported in ANSYS Mechanical. Not a problem, you just need to define it in APDL and put it in a command object. In this example we do a very simple temperature dependent material:

```
!    Commands inserted into this file will be executed just after material
definitions in /PREP7.
!    The material number for this body is equal to the parameter "matid".

!    Active UNIT system in Workbench when this object was created:  U.S.
Customary (in, lbm, lbf, s, V, A)
!======================================================== SNIP
mptemp,1,30,50,600,700
mpdata,dens,matid,1,.0007,.00069,.00066,.00065
mpdata,ex,matid,1,29e6 ,28.9e6,28.5e6,27e6
!======================================================== SNIP
```

See how it defines the material ID at the start of the code. Each body in your model will have a unique ID and ANSYS Mechanical will put that ID with a *set command in the command object for you. Now you just use "matid" to reference it. Also note that you can use comments to clearly show where your code is. This is useful for when you may want to search the input file that it gets put in to.

This is what the material definition looks like in the input file generated by ANSYS Mechanical:

```
MP,NUXY,1,0.3,
MP,MURX,1,10000,
```

```
/wb,mat,end                 !  done sending materials
! ****** Begin Command Snippet ******
*set,matid,1
!   Commands inserted into this file will be executed just after material
definitions in /PREP7.
!   The material number for this body is equal to the parameter "matid".

!   Active UNIT system in Workbench when this object was created:  U.S.
Customary (in, lbm, lbf, s, V, A)
!========================================================= ERMSNIP
mptemp,1,30,50,600,700
mpdata,dens,matid,1,.0007,.00069,.00066,.00065
mpdata,ex,matid,1,29e6 ,28.9e6,28.5e6,27e6
!========================================================= ERMSNIP

! ****** End  Command Snippet ******
!*********************** Model Summary *******************
```

MATID also refers to the REAL and TYPE so you can change real constants, sections, or element types the same way.

13.4   Interacting with APDL Command Objects

There are many ways in ANSYS Mechanical to interact with the APDL Command Objects that you insert into the tree. Besides the input tab where you enter your APDL script, you can use the Right Mouse Button and change values in the Details View of the object.

If you Right Mouse Button on an object, you get a context menu that lets you do many useful things like duplicating, copy, cut, delete, and rename. One of the best options in the menu is Suppress. This allows the user to turn a APDL script off without deleting it.

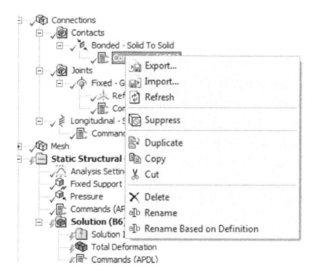

Figure 13.5: Right Mouse Button Menu

The detail view for a command object is important because it allows the user to not only see what files are attached to the object, but also control suppression and define what type of command is in the object. However, the most important part of the details view is that it provides the mechanism for passing parameters back and forth.

For PREP command objects, the user can specify up to 9 arguments that get passed to your APDL macro, and those arguments can be managed ANSYS Mechanical parameters. This opens up a large number of possibilities.

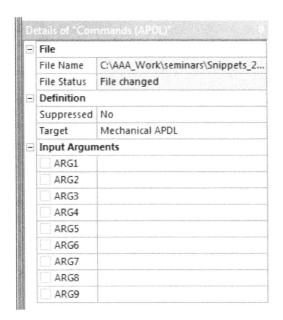

Figure 13.6: PREP Command Object Details Dialog

POST command objects not only let you pass parameters to the solver, but you can also bring parameters back. In the definition section you can define a prefix, and any ANSYS Mechanical APDL parameter that is created with that prefix will be passed back and displayed in the detail view. The default my_ works just fine.

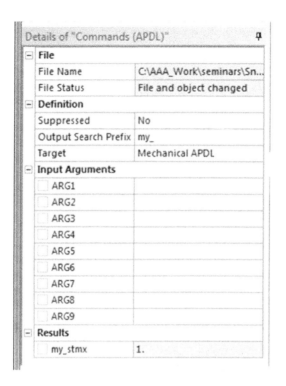

Figure 13.7: POST Command Object Details Dialog

Note: the program only looks for parameters to bring back that are created a POST command object. So if you want a parameter that is created in a PREP or ITEM command object, you need to add a POST command object that simply assigns the parameter to itself in that object.

As an example, if you want to return a parameter you created in a macro that applies some load you would do the following.

In the PREP Command Object:

```
! ... bunch of code above this part
! Find out the max Z value, we will want to know what that is later
*get,my_mxz,node,,mxloc,z
! ...more code for your macro below
```

In the POST Command Object

```
my_mxz = my_mxz
```

That is all it takes.

Here is an example where a macro is used to get the participation factors from a modal analysis and brings them back:

```
*set,last
```

```
*get,my_nmd,active,,set,sbst
*get,my_pf01,mode, 1,pfact
*get,my_pf02,mode, 2,pfact
*get,my_pf03,mode, 3,pfact
*get,my_pf04,mode, 4,pfact
*get,my_pf05,mode, 5,pfact
*get,my_pf06,mode, 6,pfact
*get,my_pf07,mode, 7,pfact
*get,my_pf08,mode, 8,pfact
*get,my_pf09,mode, 9,pfact
*get,my_pf10,mode,10,pfact
*get,my_pf11,mode,11,pfact
*get,my_pf12,mode,12,pfact
```

Produces:

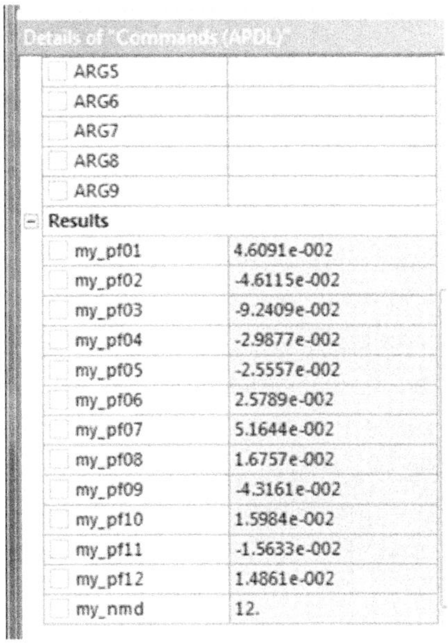

Details of "Commands (APDL)"	
ARG5	
ARG6	
ARG7	
ARG8	
ARG9	
Results	
my_pf01	4.6091e-002
my_pf02	-4.6115e-002
my_pf03	-9.2409e-002
my_pf04	-2.9877e-002
my_pf05	-2.5557e-002
my_pf06	2.5789e-002
my_pf07	5.1644e-002
my_pf08	1.6757e-002
my_pf09	-4.3161e-002
my_pf10	1.5984e-002
my_pf11	-1.5633e-002
my_pf12	1.4861e-002
my_nmd	12.

Figure 13.8: Results from Participation Factor Command Object

Simple parameters work great, but ou cannot pass arrays or strings back and forth. Also, you cannot create parameter names on the fly by embedding a parameter in the parameter name: *get,my_pf%i% does not work.

13.5   Referring to entities in a Command Object

As mentioned above, if you assign a command object to an actual entity in the model tree, a parameter is established that your macro can us to refer to that entity. But what do you do for more general APDL code that needs to work with other entities in your model or on entities that you select? You have two options.

The first option, and the old-school method, is to use APDL selection logic to get at the entities you want. Using *GET and other APDL tools you can interrogate the model and select entities that way. An example would be wanting to find out what node is at the largest radius in a model and do some calculation on the results on that node. This is a common *GET and NSEL command sequence.

A more modern approach is to do that work in ANSYS Mechanical and use names selections. Any named selection in ANSYS Mechanical get passed as components to ANSYS Mechanical APDL. Some users even place additional information in the name that they can parse with ADPL to do more complex operations. An example would be applying a load that is not supported in ANSYS Mechanical. Assign a names selection with a name that tells your APDL script what type of load it is and the magnitude. Maybe you are running a voltage-thermal-structural solve from ANSYS Mechanical. You can apply voltage as voltage_132 as a named selection on the surface you want to apply the voltage to. Your macro would loop through all the named selections, find ones that start with "voltage" and assign the value after the _ as the voltage.

Do remember that no geometry is passed to the solver. The input file will contain node or element components based on the named selection you assign to the geometry that contains the nodes or elements.

13.6   Using APDL Command Objects to Create Plots

Another fantastic capability available with command objects is the ability to use the plotting functions in ANSYS Mechanical APDL and bring the plots you create back to ANSYS Mechanical and have them placed in the tree. If you create a PNG file with an APDL command object, that PNG file is detected by ANSYS Mechanical and added to the tree under as part of the command object. This is very useful for post processing a model that may not be supported in the ANSYS Mechanical Post Processing or for creating standard plots using scripting.

The key to using this feature is to use the /SHOW,PNG command in your APDL script. Everything else is standard APDL.

As an example, the following APDL commands make a single plot showing multiple mode shapes:

```
set,last
/gfile,600
/show,png
*get,nmd,active,,set,sbst
icc = 1
irr = 1
np = 3
aa = 2.8/np
```

```
bb = 1.9/np
xx = -1
yy = 1-bb
/plopts,info,0
/plopts,minm,0
/psymb,cs,off
/triad,off
/view,1,.9875,.125,-.09
/angle,1,-50.41
/dist,1,11
/focus,1,.386,1.192,10
/RGB,INDEX,100,100,100, 0
/RGB,INDEX, 80, 80, 80,13
/RGB,INDEX, 60, 60, 60,14
/RGB,INDEX, 0, 0, 0,15
*do,i,1,nmd
    set,1,i
    *get,frq,mode,i,freq
    /window,1,xx,xx+aa,yy,yy+bb
    /ANUM ,0,     1,-0.85480     , 0.37396
    /TSPEC, 15, 0.75,   1, 359,   0
    /TLAB,xx+.05,yy+.05,'%i%: %frq%'

    plnsol,u,sum
    /annot,delete

    /noerase
    xx = xx + aa
    icc = icc + 1
    *if,icc,gt,np,then
        xx = -1
        yy = yy - bb
        icc = 1
        irr = irr + 1
    *endif
    *if,irr,gt,np,then
        /erase
        /annot,delete
        icc = 1
        irr = 1
        xx = -1
        yy = 1 - bb
    *endif
 *enddo
/erase
/annot,delete
```

```
/win,1,full
/show,close
```

Executing this command objects results in the following image attached to your model Tree. There were 20 modes extracted from this simple model, so three blots were appended.

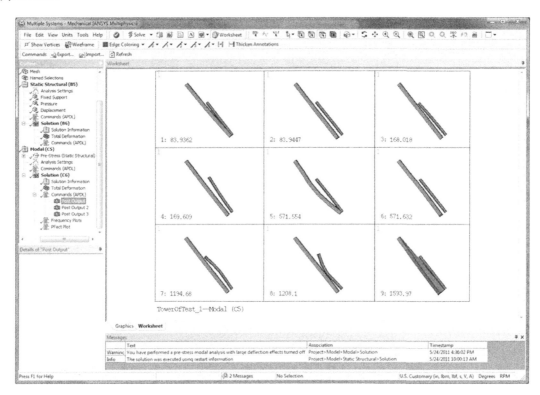

Figure 13.9: PNG Blot from ANSYS Mechanical APDL in the ANSYS Mechanical Tree

Another similar need is to make graphs of results in ANSYS Mechanical APDL. This simple command object creates a bar graph showing participation factors:

```
*set,last
*get,nmd,active,,set,sbst
*dim,pfs,,nmd
*do,ii,1,nmd
  *get,pfs(ii),mode,ii,pfact
*enddo
/show,png
/gropt,fill,1
/xrange,0,nmd+1
/gropt,divx,nmd+1
/axlab,x,'Mode'
/axlab,y,'PFact'
*vplot,,pfs(1)
/show,close
```

And this is what shows up in your ANSYS Mechanical model:

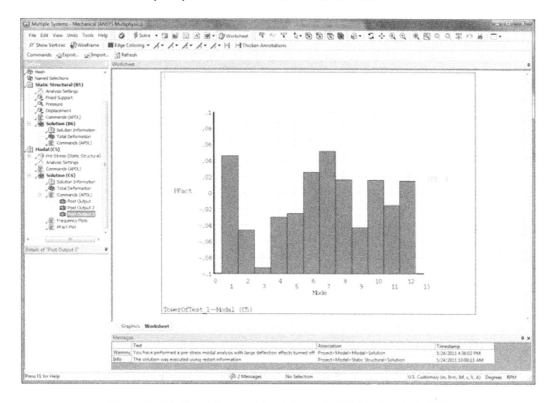

Figure 13.10: Graph brought back from ANSYS Mechanical APDL

Chapter 14: APDL Final Exam

14.1 Water Tower Macro

To finish up this book we present a simple "vertical application" written in Tcl/Tk. It constructs the geometry for an axi-symmetric water tower. Although not a sophisticated work of programming art, it is a simple overview of everything covered in this book, and we recommend that readers take their time to work their way through it to reinforce what they have learned.

Using APDL, create a macro to generate the water tower shown below.

Default parameter values are as follows:

r_t = 10 feet   h = 50 feet

t_t = 6 inches   theta = 60 degrees

r_s = 5 feet h_w = 15 feet

t_s = 8 inches   rho = 0.0362 lb_m/in^3

r_g = 9 feet

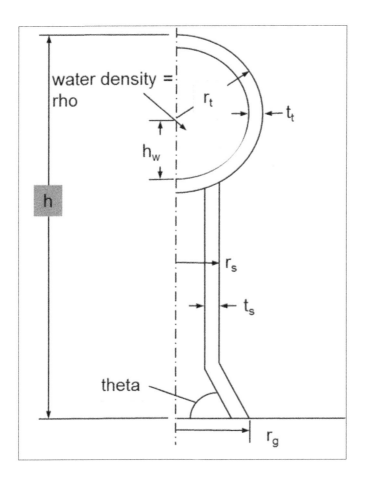

To reinforce the lessons learned, the instructions are only a guide and are missing information. You will need to define variables as needed, understand each command line, locate the commands within your macro file, etc.

Begin your macro with:

```
FINISH
/CLEAR
```

As you are working, execute your script frequently to verify its proper execution. Remember, writing APDL is like any other computer code: expect bugs that are challenging to find. Have fun and good luck!

14.1.1 Water Tower Geometry

1: The first step is to define default parameters as listed above. Rather than converting feet to inches throughout the macro, it will be easier to include a section where parameters in feet are converted to parameters in inches. Underneath the parameter definitions, insert the following:

```
Rt=Rt*12 ! Tank outer radius (inches)
Rs=Rs*12 ! Support O.R. (inches)
Rg=Rg*12 ! Base O.R. @ ground (inches)
H=H*12   ! Watertower height (inches)
Hw=Hw*12 ! Height of water (inches)
```

2: Create the main support area as a rectangle (be sure to enter the preprocessor).

```
/PREP7
RECTNG,rs-ts,rs,0,h-rt
```

3: Offset the Working Plane by r_g and rotate so that the Working Plane y-axis is at an angle, theta, to the "ground."

```
WPOFFS,rg
WPROTAT,90-theta
```

4: Create the angled base area as a rectangle with a height of $2r_g$.

```
RECTNG,-ts,0,0,2*rg
```

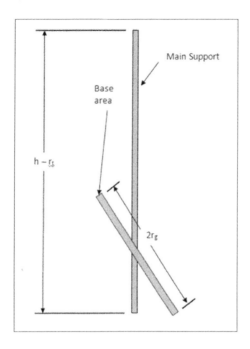

5: Create a line extending from the Global Cartesian origin to the lower right hand corner of the base area. This will be used to divide the base area at the "ground."

```
K        !Default location=0,0,0
L,KP(0,0,0),KP(rg,0,0)
```

6: Divide the base area by the line and partition the areas.

```
ASBL,2,9
APTN,all
```

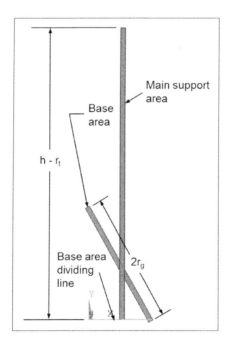

7: Delete the unused areas and their associated lines and keypoints as indicated in the
    figure.

```
ADEL,2,3,1,1
ADEL,6,,,1
```

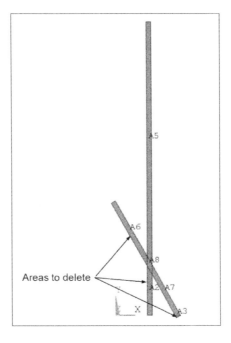

8: Add the remaining areas together to make a single area.

```
AADD,all
```

9: Realign the working plane with the global cartesian, then offset the Working Plane to
    the location of the center of the tank.

```
WPLANE,,0,0,0
WPOFFS,,h-rt
```

10: Create the annulus as shown.

```
CYL4,0,0,rt-tt,-90,rt,90
```

11: Divide the support area by the outer radius line of the tank.

```
ASBL,1,1
```

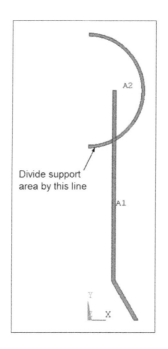

12: Delete the resulting unused area and its associated lines and keypoints.

```
ADEL,3,,,1
```

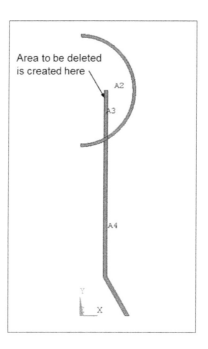

13: Glue the remaining two areas together.

```
AGLUE,all
```

14: Create a line at the water level in the tank. Note how the L command uses inline kp() functions to get the keypoint numbers by location:

```
K,,,h-2*rt+tt+hw
K,,rt,h-2*rt+tt+hw
```

```
L,kp(0,h-2*rt+tt+hw,0),kp(rt,h-2*rt+tt+hw,0)
```

15: Divide the inner radius arc of the tank by the line created in the previous step. This will create a line to which the water pressure can be applied.

```
LSBL,4,1
```

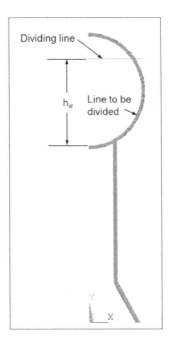

14.1.2 Water Tower Attributes

16: Define the Element Type: Axisymmetric 8-node plane elements

```
ET,1,plane82,,,1
```

17: The default material properties need to be defined as parameters. Use these values as the default:

– Tank - Steel
- $E = 29 \times 10^6$ psi
- $\upsilon = 0.27$
- $\alpha = 8.8 \times 10^{-6}$ /ºF
- $k = 9$ Btu/hr•ft•ºF

```
MP,ex,1,Et
MP,nuxy,1,nut
MP,alpx,1,alphat
MP,kxx,1,kt/(3600*12)
```

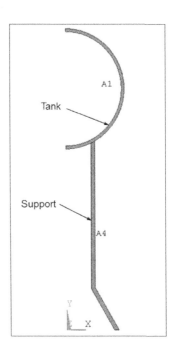

– Support – Concrete
- $E = 4.5$ ksi
- $\upsilon = 0.15$

- $\alpha = 6 \times 10^{-6}$ /ºF
- $k = 0.17$ Btu/hr•ft•ºF

```
MP,ex,2,Es
MP,nuxy,2,nus
MP,alpx,2,alphas
MP,kxx,2,ks/(3600*12)
```

18: The next step is to specify parametric mesh sizes. You want to size elements so that the number of divisions across the component having the minimum thickness (tank or support) is 2. Using the parameters you have results in:

```
ESIZE,min(Tt,Ts)/(1.1)
```

19: Since we know the keypoint numbers, we can force a nice mapped mesh by defining the mapped area using keypoint corners:

```
AMAP,4,10,6,8,14
AMAP,1,7,1,2,5
```

14.1.3 Water Tower Loading

20: There is no valid reason to do this, but the obsessive compulsive nature that lurks within all engineers leads us to clean things up by compressing the node numbers:

```
NUMCMP,NODE
```

21: To start specifying loads, it is better to enter the Solution Processor. You can do it in PREP7 but you should do it in /SOLU:

```
FINI
/SOLU
```

22: The first step is to attach the tower to the ground by rigidly constraining the line at the base of the water tower

```
LSEL,S,LOC,Y,0
DL,ALL,,ALL
ALLSEL,ALL
```

23: We now want to apply a pressure load onto the nodes on the inner surface of the water tank. This can be done more easily by using more modern commands than those used here, but we want to force the usage of a "helper" macro to select those nodes.

- Create a second text file called nodewater.mac and place the following code within it:

```
!Define and activate local cylindrical coordinate system (11)
at center of tank
LOCAL,11,1,,H-RT          !Define CS 11
CSYS,11

!Calculate parameters for convenience
RIT=RT-TT                 !Inner radius of tank
ALPHA=90+ASIN((HW-RIT)/RIT)
!Angle between horizontal and intersection of tank
!and waterline in CS 11

!Apply varying pressure (between 0 and rho*g*hw) to line
!Select all lines along inner radius of tank

LSEL,S,LOC,X,RIT
LSEL,R,LOC,Y,-90,ASIN((HW-RIT)/RIT)  !Reselect line between
bottom of tank and waterline
NSLL,,1
RIT=
ALPHA=
CSYS,0
```

- Save the file in your working directory so you can call it from the main macro.

- We recommend that you study the nodewater macro to understand the operations it is performing.

24: Using a table, apply pressure along the inside of the tank equal to rho×g×x where g=1 (the water tower is located on earth) and x is defined as shown in the illustration. A macro which selects nodes subject to water pressure, nodewater.mac, has been pre-written for you. Call this macro before applying the pressure. Select everything after applying the loads

```
NODEWATER
*DIM,PRESTAB,TABLE,2,,,Y
PRESTAB(1,0)=H-2*RT+TT,H-2*RT+HW+TT
PRESTAB(0,1)=0,RHO*HW,0
SF,ALL,PRESS,%PRESTAB%
ALLSEL
```

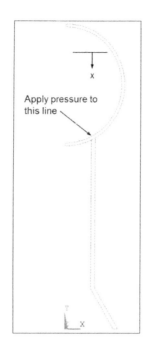

25: For the temperature profile, we are going to exercise the use of a table array. Define the y-locations as a fraction of height, then convert to actual height using *VOPER on the zeroeth column.

```
*DIM,TEMPTAB,TABLE,5,,,Y
TEMPTAB(1,0)=0,0.25,0.5,0.75,1
TEMPTAB(0,1)=0,130,110,75,35,4
*VOPER,TEMPTAB(1,0),TEMPTAB(1,0),MULT,H
BF,ALL,TEMP,%TEMPTAB%
```

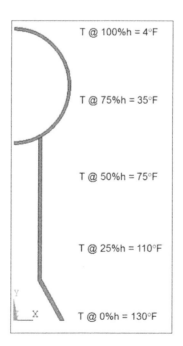

14.1.4 Water Tower Solution and Results

The macro should now build, mesh, define, constrain, and load your model. All that is left is to solve it and post process.

26: Solve the model

```
SOLVE
```

27: To really understand the results we want to grab the displacement in X, Y, and SUM for all of the nodes:

```
SOLVE
/POST1
*DIM,DISPS,,ndinqr(0,14),3
*VGET,DISPS(1,1),NODE,1,U,X
*VGET,DISPS(1,2),NODE,1,U,Y
```

28: But, since there is no *VGET for USUM, we will have to use a *DO loop and math operations to fill in the third column of the array. Do note that this can be done with a vector operation instead of a *DO loop.

```
*DO,i,1,ndinqr(0,14)
        DISPS(i,3)=SQRT(DISPS(i,1)**2+DISPS(i,2)**2)
*ENDDO
```

29: To find out the max displacement, use *VSCFUN to get the max USUM.

```
*VSCFUN,usum_max,MAX,DISPS(1,3)
```

30: Write the displacements and maximum total displacements to the file towerdisps.txt. Although FORTRAN descriptors are used below, feel free to use C descriptors if you wish.

```
*CFOPEN,towerdisps,txt
*VWRITE,usum_max
('Maximum total displacement = ',F6.4)
*VWRITE
(' ')
*VWRITE
('Nodal Displacements:')
*VWRITE
(' ')
*VWRITE
(' Node',2X,'X-Disps',2X,'Y-Disps',4X,'Total')
*VWRITE
```

```
('-----',2X,'-------',2X,'-------',3X,'------')
*VWRITE,SEQU,DISPS(1,1),DISPS(1,2),DISPS(1,3)
(F5.0,3F9.4)
*CFCLOSE
```

If you plot the results, they should look something like this, with pressure and temperature loads shown:

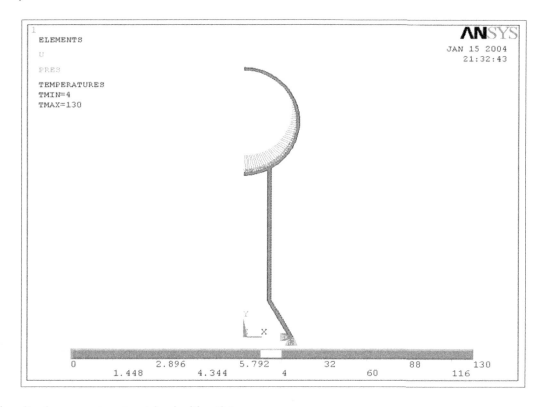

The displacement output looks like this:

```
towerdisps.txt - Notepad

File  Edit  Format  View  Help

Maximum total displacement = 0.4513

Nodal Displacements:

Node   X-Disps   Y-Disps     Total
----   -------   -------    ------
  1.    0.0536    0.1745    0.1825
  2.    0.0255    0.3901    0.3910
  3.    0.0534    0.1773    0.1852
  4.    0.0532    0.1801    0.1878
  5.    0.0530    0.1829    0.1904
  6.    0.0528    0.1856    0.1930
  7.    0.0526    0.1884    0.1956
  8.    0.0525    0.1911    0.1982
  9.    0.0523    0.1938    0.2008
 10.    0.0522    0.1966    0.2034
 11.    0.0520    0.1993    0.2059
 12.    0.0519    0.2019    0.2085
 13.    0.0517    0.2046    0.2111
 14.    0.0516    0.2073    0.2136
 15.    0.0514    0.2099    0.2162
 16.    0.0513    0.2126    0.2187
 17.    0.0511    0.2152    0.2212
 18.    0.0509    0.2178    0.2237
 19.    0.0507    0.2205    0.2262
 20.    0.0505    0.2231    0.2287
 21.    0.0503    0.2257    0.2312
 22.    0.0501    0.2282    0.2337
 23.    0.0499    0.2308    0.2361
 24.    0.0496    0.2334    0.2386
 25.    0.0494    0.2359    0.2410
 26.    0.0491    0.2385    0.2435
 27.    0.0489    0.2410    0.2459
 28.    0.0486    0.2435    0.2483
 29.    0.0483    0.2460    0.2507
 30.    0.0480    0.2485    0.2531
 31.    0.0477    0.2509    0.2554
 32.    0.0474    0.2534    0.2578
```

End of Workshop

14.1.5 Doing More

Although this is the end of the workshop, it does not have to be the end of your macro. We recommend the following exercises to practice your skills:

- Use *ASK to prompt the user for the input parameters
- Use UIDL to create a command in the GUI with dialog boxes to:
    o Prompt the user for parameters
    o Run the model
    o Display Results
- Add commands to automate the post processing
- Add a prestressed modal analysis
- Add a PSD (maybe an earthquake) to the solution sequence
- Hook the macro up to an external optimization tool

Appendix 1: Inquiry Functions

Nodes

ndinqr(node,key)

> node - node number, or 0 for key = 12, 13, 14, 16
> key - information needed
>   = 1, select status
>   = 12, number of defined nodes
>   = 13, number of selected nodes
>   = 14, highest node number defined
>   = 16, next available node number
>   = -2, superelement flag
>   = -3, master degrees of freedom bit pattern
>   = -4, active degrees of freedom bit pattern
>   = -5, solid model attachment
>   = -6, pack nodal line parametric value
> output arguments:
> for key = 1
>   = 0, node is undefined.
>   = -1, node is unselected.
>   = 1, node is selected.

Elements

elmiqr(ielem,key)

> ielem - element number, or 0 for key = 12, 13, 14, 16
> key - information needed
>   = 1, select status
>   = 12, number of defined elements
>   = 13, number of selected elements
>   = 14, highest element number defined
>   = 16, next available element number
>   = -1, material number
>   = -2, type
>   = -3, real
>   = -4, element section ID number
>   = -5, coordinate system number
>   = -7, solid model reference
> output arguments:
> for key = 1
>   = 0, element is undefined.

= -1, element is unselected.

= 1, element is selected.

Keypoints

kpinqr(kpid,key)

kpid - keypoint number, or 0 for key = 12, 13, 14,16

key - information needed

= 1, select status

= 12, number of defined keypoints

= 13, number of selected keypoints

= 14, highest keypoint number defined

= 16, next available keypoint number

= -1, material number

= -2, type

= -3, real

= -4, attached node number, if meshed

= -7, attached element number, if meshed

output arguments:

for key = 1

= 0, undefined.

= -1, unselected.

= 1, selected.

Lines

lsinqr(lsid,key)

lsid - line number, or 0 for key = 12, 13, 14,16

key - information needed

= 1, select status (same output arguments)

= 2, length (in model units)

= 12, number of defined lines

= 13, number of selected lines

= 14, highest line number defined

= 16, next available line number

= -1, material number

= -2, type

= -3, real

= -4, number of nodes

= -5, element coordinate system number

= -6, number of elements

= -7, solid model reference

= -8, number of element divs in existing mesh

= -9, attached keypoint 1

= -10, attached keypoint 2

= -15, section ID

= -16, number of element divs for next mesh

= -17, 0 = hard / 1 = soft NDIV

= -18, 0 = hard / 1 = soft SPACE

Areas

aringr(areaid,key)

areaid - area number, or 0 for key = 12, 13, 14, 16

key - information needed

= 1, select status

= 12, number of defined areas

= 13, number of selected areas

= 14, highest area number defined

= 16, next available area number

= -1, material number

= -2, type

= -3, real

= -4, number of attached nodes, if meshed

= -6, number of attached elements, if meshed

= -7, pointer to area in foreign db

= -8, element shape

= -9, midside node element key

= -10, element coordinate system

= -11, area constraint information

Volumes

vlingr(vnmi,key)

vnmi - volume number, or 0 for key = 12, 13, 14, 16

key - information needed

= 1, select status

= 12, number of defined volumes

= 13, number of selected volumes

= 14, highest volume number defined

= 16, next available volume number

= -1, material number

= -2, type

= -3, real

= -4, number of attached nodes, if meshed

= -6, number of attached elements, if meshed

= -8, element shape
= -9, midside node element key
= -10, element coordinate system

output arguments:
for key = 1
= 0, undefined.
= -1, unselected.
= 1, selected.

Element Types

etyiqr(itype,key)

itype – element type number, 0 for key = 12, 14, 16
key - information needed
= 1, select status
= 12, number of defined element types
= 14, highest element type number defined
= 16, next available element type

Real Constants

rlinqr(nreal,key)

nreal – real constant number, 0 for key = 12, 13, 14,16
key - information needed
= 1, select status
= 12, number of defined real constants
= 13, number of selected real constants
= 14, highest real constant number defined
= 16, next available real constant

Section Tables

sectinqr(nsect,key)

nsect – section ID number, 0 for key = 12, 13, 14,16
key - information needed
= 1, select status
= 12, number of defined section IDs
= 13, number of selected section IDs
= 14, highest section number defined
= 16, next available section

Material Properties

mpinqr(mat,iprop,key)

    mat - material number, or 0 for key = 12, 14,16

    iprop – 0 to test for existence of any material property with number mat or EX = 1, EY = 2, EZ = 3, NUXY = 4, NUYZ = 5, NUXZ = 6, GXY = 7, GYZ = 8, GXZ = 9, ALPX = 10, ALPY = 11, ALPZ = 12, DENS = 13, MU =14, DAMP = 15, KXX = 16, KYY = 17, KZZ = 18, RSVX = 19, RSVY = 20, RSVZ = 21, C = 22, HF =23, VISC = 24, EMIS = 25, ENTH = 26, LSST = 27, PRXY = 28, PRYZ = 29, PRXZ = 30, MURX = 31, MURY = 32, MURZ = 33, PERX = 34, PERY = 35, PERZ = 36, MGXX = 37, MGYY = 38, MGZZ = 39, EGXX = 40, EGYY = 41, EGZZ = 42, TGXX = 43, TGYY = 44, TGZZ = 45, SONC = 46, SLIM = 47, ELIM = 48, ORTH = 54, CABL = 55, RIGI = 56, HGLS = 57, BM = 58, QRAT = 59, REFT = 60, PLAS = 61, CREE = 62, FAIL = 63, BH = 64, PIEZ = 65, SWEL = 66, WATE = 67, CONC = 68, PFLO = 69, ANEL = 70, ACOU = 71, EVIS = 72, USER = 73, NL = 74, HYPE = 75, NNEW = 76, MOON = 77, OGDE = 78, SUTH = 79, WIND = 80

    key - information needed
     = 1, select status
     = 12, number of defined material properties
     = 14, highest material property number defined
     = 16, next available material property number

Constraint Equations

Constraint Equations ceinqr(ceid,key)

    ceid – constraint eq. number, 0 for key = 12, 13, 14, 16
    key - information needed
     = 1, select status
     = 12, number of defined constraint equations
     = 13, number of selected constraint equations
     = 14, highest constraint equation defined
     = 16, next available constraint equation
     = -1, master DOF for this constraint equation

Couples

cpinqr(cpid,key)

    cpid – coupled set number, 0 for key = 12, 13, 14,16
    key - information needed
     = 1, select status
     = 12, number of defined coupled sets
     = 13, number of selected coupled sets
     = 14, highest coupled set number defined

= 16, next available coupled set

Coordinate System

csyiqr(csysid,key)

      csysid – coordinate system number, 0 for key = 12, 13, 14, 16
      key - information needed
        = 1, select status
        = 12, number of defined coordinate systems
        = 14, highest coordinate system number used
        = 16, next available coordinate system

Warnings and Error Messages

erinqr(key)

      key - information needed
        = 3, total number of notes displayed
        = 4, total number of warnings displayed
        = 5, total number of errors displayed
        = 6, total number of fatal errors displayed

Appendix 2: Completed Workshop Macros

Workshop 1: bracket1.mac

```
!!!!!!!!!!!!!!!!!!!!!!!!!!!!!!!!!!!
!                                 !
!          bracket1.mac           !
!           Written by            !
!          Jeffrey Strain         !
!    Updated November 10, 2003    !
!                                 !
!  This file accomplishes the     !
!  objectives of Workshop 1 of    !
!  the ANSYS APDL and             !
!  Customization class.           !
!                                 !
!!!!!!!!!!!!!!!!!!!!!!!!!!!!!!!!!!!
fini
/clear

/PREP7
K,1,0,0,0,
K,2,0.25,0,0,
K,3,0.25,4-.25,0,
K,4,3,4-.25,0,
K,5,3,4,0,
K,6,0,4,0,
L,        1,        6
L,        6,        5
L,        2,        3
L,        3,        4
!*
LFILLT,1,2,.1+.25, ,
!*
LFILLT,3,4,.1, ,

A,1,2,9,10,4,5,8,7

VEXT,ALL, , ,0,0,4,,,,

KWPAVE,5,17
wprot,0,-90,0
CYL4, , ,1, , , ,-.25
VSBV,         1,         2
!*
ET,1,SOLID92
!*
!*
!*
MPTEMP,,,,,,,,
MPTEMP,1,0
MPDATA,EX,1,,29e6
MPDATA,PRXY,1,,.27
ESIZE,0.25/2,0,
MSHAPE,1,3D
MSHKEY,0
!*
VMESH,ALL
!*
FINISH
/SOL
FLST,2,1,5,ORDE,1
FITEM,2,3
!*
/GO
DA,P51X,ALL,
ASEL,S, , ,         7
NSLA,S,1
```

```
!*
*GET,NUMNODE,NODE,,COUNT, , , ,
!*
/GO
F,ALL,FY,-100/NUMNODE
ALLSEL,ALL
SBCTRAN
EPLOT
FINISH
```

Workshop 2: bracket2.mac

```
!!!!!!!!!!!!!!!!!!!!!!!!!!!!!!!!!!!
!                                 !
!           bracket2.mac          !
!            Written by           !
!          Jeffrey Strain         !
!     Updated November 10, 2003   !
!                                 !
!   This file accomplishes the    !
!   objectives of Workshop 2 of   !
!   the ANSYS APDL and            !
!   Customization class.          !
!                                 !
!!!!!!!!!!!!!!!!!!!!!!!!!!!!!!!!!!!
!Clear database
fini
/clear

!Define parameters
Elemtype=92     !Element type
Eb=29e6 !Young's Modulus for bracket
Nub=0.27        !Poisson's ratio for bracket
Force=100       !Load on bracket
Rb=0.1 !Bend radius
W=3             !Bracket width
D=3             !Bracket depth
H=4             !Bracket height
Rh=1.0 !Hole radius
T=0.25 !Bracket thickness

!Create bracket geometry
/PREP7
K,1,0,0,0,
K,2,T,0,0,
K,3,T,H-T,0,
K,4,W,H-T,0,
K,5,W,H,0,
K,6,0,H,0,
L,        1,        6
L,        6,        5
L,        2,        3
L,        3,        4
!*
LFILLT,1,2,Rb+T, ,
!*
LFILLT,3,4,Rb, ,

A,1,2,9,10,4,5,8,7

VEXT,ALL, , ,0,0,D,,,,

KWPAVE,5,17
wprot,0,-90,0
CYL4, , ,1, , , , ,-T
VSBV,        1,        2
!*
ET,1,elemtype
!*
!*
```

```
!*
MPTEMP,,,,,,,
MPTEMP,1,0
MPDATA,EX,1,,Eb
MPDATA,PRXY,1,,Nub
ESIZE,T/2,0,
MSHAPE,1,3D
MSHKEY,0
!*
VMESH,ALL
!*
FINISH
/SOL
FLST,2,1,5,ORDE,1
FITEM,2,3
!*
/GO
DA,P51X,ALL,
ASEL,S, , ,          7
NSLA,S,1
!*
*GET,NUMNODE,NODE,,COUNT, , , ,
!*
/GO
F,ALL,FY,-Force/NUMNODE
ALLSEL,ALL
SBCTRAN
EPLOT
FINISH
```

Workshop 3: bracket3.mac

```
!!!!!!!!!!!!!!!!!!!!!!!!!!!!!!!!!!!!
!                                  !
!           bracket3.mac           !
!           Written by             !
!         Jeffrey Strain           !
!     Updated November 10, 2003    !
!                                  !
!  This file accomplishes the      !
!  objectives of Workshop 3 of     !
!  the ANSYS APDL and              !
!  Customization class.            !
!                                  !
!!!!!!!!!!!!!!!!!!!!!!!!!!!!!!!!!!!!
!Clear database
fini
/clear

!Define parameters
Elemtype=92      !Element type
Eb=29e6          !Young's Modulus for bracket
Nub=0.27         !Poisson's ratio for bracket
Force=100        !Load on bracket
Rb=0.1           !Bend radius
W=3              !Bracket width
D=3              !Bracket depth
H=4              !Bracket height
Rh=1.0           !Hole radius
T=0.25           !Bracket thickness

MULTIPRO,'START',4
       *CSET,1,3,W,'ENTER WIDTH',W
       *CSET,4,6,H,'ENTER HEIGHT',H
       *CSET,7,9,D,'ENTER DEPTH',D
       *CSET,10,12,RB,'ENTER BEND RADIUS',RB
MULTIPRO,'END'

*ASK,Rh,radius of hole,%Rh%
*ASK,T,thickness of bracket,%T%
```

```
!Create bracket geometry
/PREP7
K,1,0,0,0,
K,2,T,0,0,
K,3,T,H-T,0,
K,4,W,H-T,0,
K,5,W,H,0,
K,6,0,H,0,
L,       1,       6
L,       6,       5
L,       2,       3
L,       3,       4
!*
LFILLT,1,2,Rb+T, ,
!*
LFILLT,3,4,Rb, ,

A,1,2,9,10,4,5,8,7

VEXT,ALL, , ,0,0,D,,,,

KWPAVE,5,17
wprot,0,-90,0
CYL4, , ,1, , , ,-T
VSBV,        1,        2
!*
ET,1,elemtype
!*
!*
!*
MPTEMP,,,,,,,,
MPTEMP,1,0
MPDATA,EX,1,,Eb
MPDATA,PRXY,1,,Nub
ESIZE,T/2,0,
MSHAPE,1,3D
MSHKEY,0
!*
VMESH,ALL
!*
FINISH
/SOL
FLST,2,1,5,ORDE,1
FITEM,2,3
!*
/GO
DA,P51X,ALL,
ASEL,S, , ,        7
NSLA,S,1
!*
*GET,NUMNODE,NODE,,COUNT, , , ,
!*
/GO
F,ALL,FY,-Force/NUMNODE
ALLSEL,ALL
SBCTRAN
EPLOT
FINISH
```

Workshop 4: bracket4.mac

```
!!!!!!!!!!!!!!!!!!!!!!!!!!!!!!!!!!!
!                               !
!         bracket4.mac          !
!          Written by           !
!         Jeffrey Strain        !
!    Updated January 14, 2003   !
!                               !
!   This file accomplishes the  !
```

```
!   objectives of Workshop 4 of    !
!   the ANSYS APDL and              !
!   Customization class.            !
!                                   !
!!!!!!!!!!!!!!!!!!!!!!!!!!!!!!!!!!!!!
!Clear database
fini
/clear

*IF,arg2,LE,0,THEN
        arg2=1
*ENDIF
Rh=arg2

!Define parameters
Elemtype=92     !Element type
Eb=29e6 !Young's Modulus for bracket
Nub=0.27        !Poisson's ratio for bracket
Force=100       !Load on bracket
Rb=0.1  !Bend radius
W=3             !Bracket width
D=3             !Bracket depth
H=4             !Bracket height
T=0.25  !Bracket thickness

MULTIPRO,'START',4
        *CSET,1,3,W,'ENTER WIDTH',W
        *CSET,4,6,H,'ENTER HEIGHT',H
        *CSET,7,9,D,'ENTER DEPTH',D
        *CSET,10,12,RB,'ENTER BEND RADIUS',RB
MULTIPRO,'END'

*ASK,T,thickness of bracket,%T%

mindim=MIN(W-T-Rb,D)
*IF,2*Rh,GE,mindim,THEN
        *MSG,ERROR,2*Rh,mindim
The hole diameter of %G exceeds the minimum bracket platform%/&
dimension of %G.  Run aborted.
        mindim=
        *RETURN
*ENDIF

!Create bracket geometry
/PREP7  .
K,1,0,0,0,
K,2,T,0,0,
K,3,T,H-T,0,
K,4,W,H-T,0,
K,5,W,H,0,
K,6,0,H,0,
L,        1,        6
L,        6,        5
L,        2,        3
L,        3,        4
!*
LFILLT,1,2,Rb+T, ,
!*
LFILLT,3,4,Rb, ,

A,1,2,9,10,4,5,8,7

VEXT,ALL, , ,0,0,D,,,,

*IF,arg1,EQ,1,THEN
        KWPAVE,5,17
        wprot,0,-90,0
        CYL4, , ,Rh, , , ,-T
        VSBV,        1,        2
*ENDIF
!*
```

```
ET,1,elemtype
!*
!*
!*
MPTEMP,,,,,,,
MPTEMP,1,0
MPDATA,EX,1,,Eb
MPDATA,PRXY,1,,Nub
ESIZE,T/2,0,
MSHAPE,1,3D
MSHKEY,0
!*
VMESH,ALL
!*
FINISH
/SOL
ASEL,S,LOC,Y,0
DA,ALL,ALL,
ALLSEL

ASEL,S,LOC,X,W
NSLA,S,1
!*
*GET,NUMNODE,NODE,,COUNT, , , ,
!*
/GO
F,ALL,FY,-Force/NUMNODE
ALLSEL,ALL
SBCTRAN
EPLOT
FINISH
```

Workshop 5: bracket5a.mac

```
!!!!!!!!!!!!!!!!!!!!!!!!!!!!!!!!!
!                               !
!          bracket5a.mac        !
!            Written by         !
!          Jeffrey Strain       !
!         November 11, 2003     !
!                               !
!   This file accomplishes the  !
!   objectives of Workshop 5a of !
!   the ANSYS APDL and          !
!   Customization class.        !
!                               !
!!!!!!!!!!!!!!!!!!!!!!!!!!!!!!!!!
fini
/clear

!Set defaults
*IF,arg1,EQ,0,THEN
        arg1=1
*ENDIF
*IF,arg2,EQ,0,THEN
        arg2=.1
*ENDIF
*IF,arg3,EQ,0,THEN
        arg3=1
*ENDIF

!Parameter definitions
Elemtype=92
Eb=29e6
Nub=0.27
Force=100
Rb=0.1
W=3
D=4
```

```
H=4
T=0.25
Rh=arg2

/PREP7
K,1,0,0,0,
K,2,T,0,0,
K,3,T,H-T,0,
K,4,W,H-T,0,
K,5,W,H,0,
K,6,0,H,0,
L,         1,         6
L,         6,         5
L,         2,         3
L,         3,         4
!*
LFILLT,1,2,Rb+T, ,
!*
LFILLT,3,4,Rb, ,

A,1,2,9,10,4,5,8,7

VEXT,ALL, , ,0,0,D,,,,

KWPAVE,5,17
wprot,0,-90,0
wpoffs,(W-T-Rb)/(arg1+1)-(W-T-Rb)/2
*DO,i,1,arg1
CYL4,(i-1)*((W-T-Rb)/(arg1+1)), ,Rh, , , ,-T
*ENDDO
VSBV,          1,          ALL
!*
ET,1,elemtype
!*
!*
!*
MPTEMP,,,,,,,,
MPTEMP,1,0
MPDATA,EX,1,,Eb
MPDATA,PRXY,1,,Nub
ESIZE,T/2,0,
MSHAPE,1,3D
MSHKEY,0
!*
VMESH,ALL
!*
FINISH
/SOL
ASEL,S,LOC,Y,0
DA,ALL,ALL,
ALLSEL

!Ramp load over a series of loadsteps
*DO,j,1,arg3
ASEL,S,LOC,X,W
NSLA,S,1
*GET,NUMNODE,NODE,,COUNT, , , ,
F,ALL,FY,-Force*j/NUMNODE
ALLSEL,ALL
LSWRITE,j
*ENDDO

/pbc,all,1
/view,,1,1,1
EPLOT
FINISH
```

Workshop 5: bracket5b.mac

```
!!!!!!!!!!!!!!!!!!!!!!!!!!!!!!!!!
!                               !
!          bracket5b.mac        !
!            Written by         !
!          Jeffrey Strain       !
!          November 11, 2003    !
!                               !
!  This file accomplishes the   !
!  objectives of Workshop 5b of !
!  the ANSYS APDL and           !
!  Customization class.         !
!                               !
!!!!!!!!!!!!!!!!!!!!!!!!!!!!!!!!!!
fini
/clear

!Set defaults
*IF,arg1,EQ,0,THEN
        arg1=1
*ENDIF
*IF,arg2,EQ,0,THEN
        arg2=.1
*ENDIF
*IF,arg3,EQ,0,THEN
        arg3=1
*ENDIF

!Parameter definitions
Elemtype=92
Eb=29e6
Nub=0.27
Force=100
Rb=0.1
W=3
D=4
H=4
T=0.25
Rh=arg2

/PREP7
K,1,0,0,0,
K,2,T,0,0,
K,3,T,H-T,0,
K,4,W,H-T,0,
K,5,W,H,0,
K,6,0,H,0,
L,        1,        6
L,        6,        5
L,        2,        3
L,        3,        4
!*
LFILLT,1,2,Rb+T, ,
!*
LFILLT,3,4,Rb, ,

A,1,2,9,10,4,5,8,7

VEXT,ALL, , ,0,0,D,,,,

KWPAVE,5,17
wprot,0,-90,0
wpoffs,(W-T-Rb)/(arg1+1)-(W-T-Rb)/2

CYL4,(0:(arg1-1)*((W-T-Rb)/(arg1+1)):(W-T-Rb)/(arg1+1)), ,Rh, , , ,-T

VSBV,         1,         ALL

!*
```

```
ET,1,elemtype
!*
!*
!*
MPTEMP,,,,,,,,
MPTEMP,1,0
MPDATA,EX,1,,Eb
MPDATA,PRXY,1,,Nub
ESIZE,T/2,0,
MSHAPE,1,3D
MSHKEY,0
!*
VMESH,ALL
!*
FINISH
/SOL
ASEL,S,LOC,Y,0
DA,ALL,ALL,
ALLSEL

!Ramp load over a series of loadsteps
*DO,j,1,arg3
        ASEL,S,LOC,X,W
        NSLA,S,1
        *GET,NUMNODE,NODE,,COUNT, , , ,
        F,ALL,FY,-Force*j/NUMNODE
        ALLSEL,ALL
        LSWRITE,j
*ENDDO

/pbc,all,1
/view,,1,1,1
EPLOT
FINISH
! /EXIT,MODEL
```

Workshop 6: bracket6.mac

```
!!!!!!!!!!!!!!!!!!!!!!!!!!!!!!!!!!
!                                !
!          bracket6.mac          !
!           Written by           !
!          Jeffrey Strain        !
!       Updated March 9, 2005    !
!                                !
!   This file satisfies the      !
!   objectives of Workshop 6 of  !
!   the ANSYS APDL and           !
!   Customization class.         !
!                                !
!!!!!!!!!!!!!!!!!!!!!!!!!!!!!!!!!!
fini
/clear

!Parameter definitions
Elemtype=92
Eb=29e6
Nub=0.27
CTEb=3e-6
Force=100
Rb=0.1
W=3
D=4
H=4
T=0.25
Rh=1

/PREP7
!Create bracket geometry
```

```
K,1,0,0,0,
K,2,T,0,0,
K,3,T,H-T,0,
K,4,W,H-T,0,
K,5,W,H,0,
K,6,0,H,0,
L,        1,        6
L,        6,        5
L,        2,        3
L,        3,        4
!*
LFILLT,1,2,Rb+T, ,
!*
LFILLT,3,4,Rb, ,

A,1,2,9,10,4,5,8,7

VEXT,ALL, , ,0,0,D,,,,

KWPAVE,5,17
wprot,0,-90,0
CYL4, , ,Rh, , , ,-T
VSBV,        1,        2
!*
ET,1,elemtype
!*
!*
!*
MPTEMP,,,,,,,,
MPTEMP,1,0
MPDATA,EX,1,,Eb
MPDATA,PRXY,1,,Nub
MPDATA,ALPX,1,,CTEb
ESIZE,T,0,
MSHAPE,1,3D
MSHKEY,0
!*
VMESH,ALL
!*
FINISH
/SOL
ASEL,S,LOC,Y,0
DA,ALL,ALL,
ALLSEL
ASEL,S,LOC,X,W
NSLA,S,1
!*
*GET,NUMNODE,NODE,,COUNT, , , ,
!*
/GO
F,ALL,FY,-Force/NUMNODE
ALLSEL,ALL

!Apply temperature table
*DIM,TEMPTAB,TABLE,4,5,,X,Y
*TAXIS,TEMPTAB(1,0),1,0,.6*W,.85*W,W
*TAXIS,TEMPTAB(0,1),2,0,0.25*H,0.5*H,0.75*H,H
TEMPTAB(1,1)=600,540,450,300
TEMPTAB(1,2)=480,420,360,210
TEMPTAB(1,3)=390,360,270,180
TEMPTAB(1,4)=300,240,210,120
TEMPTAB(1,5)=240,210,150,60

BF,ALL,TEMP,%TEMPTAB%
LSWRITE,1

FDEL,ALL,ALL
BFDEL,ALL,ALL

PMAX=50
OFFST=Rb+T
```

```
*DIM,PRESTAB,TABLE,4,3,,X,Z
*TAXIS,PRESTAB(1,0),1,OFFST,OFFST+.3*(W-OFFST),OFFST+.75*(W-OFFST),W
*TAXIS,PRESTAB(0,1),2,0,0.4*D,D
PRESTAB(1,1)=.1,.3,.9,.5
PRESTAB(1,2)=.15,.4,1,.75
PRESTAB(1,3)=.09,.5,.8,.45

*TOPER,PRESTAD(1,1),PRESTAB(1,1),ADD,PRESTAB(1,1),PMAX,0,0

ASEL,,LOC,Y,H
NSLA,,1
SF,ALL,PRES,%PRESTAB%
ALLSEL
LSWRITE,2

LSSOLVE,1,2

FINI
/POST1

!Store y-deflections for each load step in a separate array
*GET,NUMNODE,NODE,,COUNT        !Obtain the number of nodes
*DO,k,1,2
        SET,k,1
        *DIM,uy_ls%k%,,NUMNODE
        *VGET,uy_ls%k%(1),NODE,1,U,Y
*ENDDO

!Add displacement vectors together
*DIM,uy_total,,NUMNODE
*VOPER,uy_total(1),uy_ls1(1),ADD,uy_ls2(1)

!Obtain max total displacement and display to user
*VABS,0,1
*VSCFUN,uy_max,MAX,uy_total(1)
*MSG,UI,uy_max
Maximum total displacement = %G

FINISH
```

Workshop 7: bracket7.mac

```
!!!!!!!!!!!!!!!!!!!!!!!!!!!!!!!!!!!
!                                 !
!            bracket7.mac         !
!             Written by          !
!          Jeffrey Strain         !
!        Updated March 9, 2005    !
!                                 !
!   This file accomplishes the    !
!   objectives of Workshop 7 of   !
!   the ANSYS APDL and            !
!   Customization class.          !
!                                 !
!!!!!!!!!!!!!!!!!!!!!!!!!!!!!!!!!!!
!Clear database
fini
/clear

!Define parameters
Elemtype=92     !Element type
Eb=29e6         !Young's Modulus for bracket
Nub=0.27        !Poisson's ratio for bracket
Force=100       !Load on bracket
Rb=0.1          !Bend radius
W=3             !Bracket width
D=3             !Bracket depth
H=4             !Bracket height
Rh=1.0          !Hole radius
```

```
T=0.25            !Bracket thickness


/PREP7

!Display the job name and user ID in the title
/INQUIRE,job,JOBNAME
/INQUIRE,userid,LOGIN
/TITLE,File %job(1)% last modified by user %userid(1)%

!Create bracket geometry
K,1,0,0,0,
K,2,T,0,0,
K,3,T,H-T,0,
K,4,W,H-T,0,
K,5,W,H,0,
K,6,0,H,0,
L,KP(0,0,0),KP(0,H,0)
L,KP(0,H,0),KP(W,H,0)
L,KP(T,0,0),KP(T,H-T,0)
L,KP(T,H-T,0),KP(W,H-T,0)
!*
LFILLT,1,2,Rb+T, ,
!*
LFILLT,3,4,Rb, ,

A,KP(0,0,0),KP(T,0,0),KP(T,H-T-RB,0),KP(T+RB,H-T,0),KP(W,H-
T,0),KP(W,H,0),KP(RB+T,H,0),KP(0,H-RB-T,0)

VEXT,ALL, , ,0,0,D,,,,

KWPAVE,KP(Rb+T,H,0),KP(W,H,D)
wprot,0,-90,0
CYL4, , ,1, , , ,-T
VSBV,         1,        2
!*
ET,1,elemtype
!*
!*
!*
MPTEMP,,,,,,,,
MPTEMP,1,0
MPDATA,EX,1,,Eb
MPDATA,PRXY,1,,Nub
ESIZE,T/2,0,
MSHAPE,1,3D
MSHKEY,0
!*
VMESH,ALL
!*
FINISH
/SOL
FLST,2,1,5,ORDE,1
FITEM,2,3
!*
/GO
DA,P51X,ALL,
ASEL,S, , ,          7
NSLA,S,1
!*
/GO
F,ALL,FY,-Force/ndinqr(0,13)
ALLSEL,ALL
SBCTRAN
EPLOT
SOLVE
FINISH
/POST1
NSORT,U,Y
*GET,uymax,SORT,0,MIN
*GET,n_uymax,SORT,0,IMIN
```

```
*MSG,UI,uymax,n_uymax
Maximum downward deflection = %G at node %I
```

Workshop 8: bracket8.mac

```
!!!!!!!!!!!!!!!!!!!!!!!!!!!!!!!!!!!!
!                                  !
!            bracket8.mac          !
!             Written by           !
!           Jeffrey Strain         !
!          November 26, 2003       !
!                                  !
!   This file satisfies the        !
!   objectives of Workshop 8 of    !
!   the ANSYS APDL and             !
!   Customization class.           !
!                                  !
!!!!!!!!!!!!!!!!!!!!!!!!!!!!!!!!!!!!
fini
/clear

!Parameter definitions
Elemtype=92
Eb=29e6
Nub=0.27
CTEb=3e-6
Force=100
Rb=0.1
W=3
D=4
H=4
T=0.25
Rh=1

/PREP7
/INQUIRE,job,JOBNAME
/INQUIRE,userid,LOGIN
/TITLE,File %job(1)% last modified by %userid(1)%
K,1,0,0,0,
K,2,T,0,0,
K,3,T,H-T,0,
K,4,W,H-T,0,
K,5,W,H,0,
K,6,0,H,0,
L,KP(0,0,0),KP(0,H,0)
L,KP(0,H,0),KP(W,H,0)
L,KP(T,0,0),KP(T,H-T,0)
L,KP(T,H-T,0),KP(W,H-T,0)
!*
LFILLT,1,2,Rb+T, ,
!*
LFILLT,3,4,Rb, ,

A,KP(0,0,0),KP(T,0,0),KP(T,H-T-RB,0),KP(T+RB,H-T,0),KP(W,H-
T,0),KP(W,H,0),KP(RB+T,H,0),KP(0,H-RB-T,0)

VEXT,ALL, , ,0,0,D,,,,

KWPAVE,KP(Rb+T,H,0),KP(W,H,D)
wprot,0,-90,0
CYL4, , ,Rh, , , ,-T
VSBV,        1,        2
!*
ET,1,elemtype
!*
!*
!*
MPTEMP,,,,,,,,
```

222

```
MPTEMP,1,0
MPDATA,EX,1,,Eb
MPDATA,PRXY,1,,Nub
MPDATA,ALPX,1,,CTEb
ESIZE,T,0,
MSHAPE,1,3D
MSHKEY,0
!*
VMESH,ALL
!*
FINISH
/SOL
ASEL,S,LOC,Y,0
DA,ALL,ALL,
ALLSEL
ASEL,S,LOC,X,W
NSLA,S,1
!*
!*
/GO
F,ALL,FY,-Force/ndinqr(0,13)
ALLSEL,ALL

!Apply temperature table
*DIM,TEMPTAB,TABLE,4,5,,X,Y
*TREAD,TEMPTAB(0,0),temperatures,txt,,3

BF,ALL,TEMP,%TEMPTAB%
LSWRITE,1

FDEL,ALL,ALL
BFDEL,ALL,ALL

PMAX=50
*DIM,PRESTAB,TABLE,4,3,,X,Z
*TREAD,PRESTAB(0,0),prescoefs,txt,,3
*TOPER,PRESTAB(1,1),PRESTAB(1,1),ADD,PRESTAB(1,1),PMAX,0,0

ASEL,,LOC,Y,H
NSLA,,1
SF,ALL,PRES,%PRESTAB%
ALLSEL
LSWRITE,2

LSSOLVE,1,2

FINI
/POST1

!Store y-deflections for each load step in a separate array
*GET,numls,ACTIVE,,SET,NSET
*DO,k,1,numls
        SET,k,1
        *DIM,uy_ls%k%,,ndinqr(0,13)
        *VGET,uy_ls%k%(1),NODE,1,U,Y
*ENDDO

!Add displacement vectors together
*DIM,uy_total,,ndinqr(0,13)
*VOPER,uy_total(1),uy_ls1(1),ADD,uy_ls2(1)

!Obtain max total displacement and display to user
*VABS,0,1
*VSCFUN,uy_max,MAX,uy_total(1)
*CFOPEN,displacements,txt
*VWRITE,uy_max
('Maximum total displacement = ',F6.4)
*VWRITE
(' ')
*VWRITE
('Nodal Displacements')
```

```
*VWRITE
(' ')
*VWRITE
('Node',2X,'Load Step 1',2X,'Load Step 2',2X,'LS1 + LS2')
*VWRITE,SEQU,uy_ls1(1),uy_ls2(1),uy_total(1)
(F4.0,2F13.4,F11.4)
*CFCLOSE

FINISH
```

Workshop 12: APDL Math, bb1.mac and ws12.mac

```
!!!!!!!!!!!!!!!!!!!!!!!!!!!!!!!!!!!!
!                                 !
!           bb1.mac               !
!          Written by             !
!        Eric Miller v            !
!        August 12, 2016          !
!                                 !
!   This file builds the simple   !
!   beam model used in Workshop   !
!   12                            !
!                                 !
!!!!!!!!!!!!!!!!!!!!!!!!!!!!!!!!!!!!
finish
/clear
/file,bb1
/PREP7
K,1,0,0,0,
K,2,0,0,10,
LSTR,          1,          2
lplot
ET,1,BEAM188
esize,1
lmesh,all
/pnum,node,1
eplot
d,1,all
f,2,fx,100
mptemp,1,0
MPDATA,EX,1,,1e6
MPDATA,PRXY,1,,.23
MPDATA,DENS,1,,.003
SECTYPE,   1, BEAM, RECT, , 0
SECOFFSET, CENT
SECDATA,.125,.125,0,0,0,0,0,0,0,0,0,0
finish
/solu
save
solve
FINISH
/POST1
plnsol,u,sum
pldisp,2


!!!!!!!!!!!!!!!!!!!!!!!!!!!!!!!!!!!!
!                                 !
!           ws12.mac              !
!          Written by             !
!        Eric Miller v            !
!        August 12, 2016          !
!                                 !
!   This file caries out the      !
!   commands in Workshop 12       !
!                                 !
!!!!!!!!!!!!!!!!!!!!!!!!!!!!!!!!!!!!

! Import a stiffness matrix
*SMAT,K1,D,IMPORT,FULL,bb1.full,STIFF
```

```
*print,K1,k1.txt
*list,k1.txt

! View the matrix as a PostScript chart
*export,K1,PS,k1.ps,COLOR

! Export in Harwell-Boeing and Matrix Market Formats and view
*export,K1,HBMAT, k1.hbmat, ascii
*export,K1,MMF, k1.mmf


! Run a modal analysis
finish
/filename,bb2
/solu
antype,2
MXPAND,5, , ,0
MODOPT,LANB,5,0,0, ,OFF
solve

! Check the orthoganality of a modal model
*SMAT,MM1,D,IMPORT,FULL,bb2.full,MASS
*SMAT,BCS1,D,IMPORT,FULL,bb2.full,NOD2BCS

*DMAT,Phi,D,IMPORT,MODE,bb2.mode
*MULT,BCS1,,Phi,,BCSPhi
*MULT,MM1,,BCSPhi,,APhi
*MULT,BCSPhi,TRANS,APhi,,mtrx1

*PRINT,mtrx1,mtrx1.txt
*list,mtrx1.txt
```

APDL Final Exam: watertower.mac

```
!!!!!!!!!!!!!!!!!!!!!!!!!!!!!!!!!!!!!!!!!!!!!!!
!                                             !
!               watertower.mac                !
!          ANSYS Macro for Calculating        !
!           Stresses in a Water Tower         !
!                   due to                    !
!     Contained Water and Thermal Gradients   !
!                                             !
!                 Created by                  !
!             Jeffrey T. Strain               !
!    Phoenix Analysis & Design Technologies   !
!              February 11, 2002              !
!         Last updated: July 30, 2004         !
!                                             !
!!!!!!!!!!!!!!!!!!!!!!!!!!!!!!!!!!!!!!!!!!!!!!!

fini
/clear

!Define geometry parameters
Rt=10               !Tank outer radius (in feet)
Tt=6                !Tank tower thickness (in inches)
Rs=5                !Support outer radius (in feet)
Ts=8                !Support thickness (in inches)
Rg=9                !Base outer radius at ground (in feet)
H=50                !Water tower height (in feet)
Theta=60            !Base angle (in degrees)

!Define loading parameters
Hw=15               !Height of water level (in feet)
Rho=.0362           !Density of water

!Define material properties
Et=29e6             !Young's modulus of tank material (psi)
```

```
nut=0.27                    !Poisson's ratio of tank material
alphat=8.8e-6               !CTE of tank material (/F)
kt=9                        !Thermal conductivity of tank material (Btu/hr-ft-F)
Es=4500          !Young's modulus of support material (psi)
nus=0.15                    !Poisson's ratio of support material
alphas=6e-6                 !CTE of support material (/F)
ks=0.17          !Thermal conductivity of suppport material (Btu/hr-ft-F)

!Convert feet to inches
Rt=Rt*12                    !Tank outer radius (in inches)
Rs=Rs*12                    !Support outer radius (in inches)
Rg=Rg*12                    !Base outer radius at ground (in inches)
H=H*12           !Water tower height (in inches)
Hw=Hw*12                    !Height of water level (in inches)

*AFUN,DEG
/PREP7

!Create support geometry:

!Create main support structure
RECTNG,rs-ts,rs,0,h-rt

!Create te base
WPOFFS,rg                 !Align working plane with base
WPROTAT,90-theta          !Rotate working plane to create base

RECTNG,-ts,0,0,2*rg    !Create rectangle to form base

!Cut base area at ground
CSYS
K
L,KP(0,0,0),KP(rg,0,0) !Create line for cutting
ASBL,2,9                              !Divide area by line

!Partition all areas and delete unused ones
APTN,all
ADEL,2,3,1,1
ADEL,6,,,1

!Combine (add) structure areas into one
AADD,all

!Create tank
WPLANE,,0,0,0           !Align tank with global cartesian
WPOFFS,,h-rt    !Offset workplane to center of tank

CYL4,0,0,rt-tt,-90,rt,90       !Create half-cylinder to form tank

!Divide support by tank and remove unused area
ASBL,1,1
ADEL,3,,,1

!Glue support to tank
AGLUE,all

!Divide inside line of tank at water level for pressure application
K,,,h-2*rt +tt+hw
K,,rt,h-2*rt+tt+hw
L,kp(0,h-2*rt+tt+hw,0),kp(rt,h-2*rt+tt+hw,0)  !Create line to divide tank
LSBL,4,1                          !Divide tank by line

!Define element type
ET,1,plane82,,,1                  !Axisymmetric 8-node plane

!Define material properties
MP,ex,1,Et                        !Define tank material properties
MP,nuxy,1,nut
MP,alpx,1,alphat
MP,kxx,1,kt/(3600*12)
```

```
MP,ex,2,Es                          !Define support properties
MP,nuxy,2,nus
MP,alpx,2,alphas
MP,kxx,2,ks/(3600*12)

!Define mesh properties
ESIZE,min(Tt,Ts)/(1.1)

!Map mesh areas by corners
AMAP,4,10,6,8,14                  !Map mesh support area
AMAP,1,7,1,2,5           !Map mesh tank area

!Compress node numbers
NUMCMP,NODE

!Exit Preprocessor and enter Solution processor
FINI
/SOLU

!Constrain water tower base at ground
LSEL,S,LOC,Y,0 !Select line at the ground (y=0)
DL,ALL,,ALL      !Contrain line in all directions
ALLSEL,ALL       !Select everything

NODEWATER        !Call nodewater.mac to select nodes subject ot water pressure
*DIM,PRESTAB,TABLE,2,,,Y
PRESTAB(1,0)=H-2*Rt+Tt,H-2*Rt+Hw+Tt
PRESTAB(0,1)=0,rho*hw,0
SF,ALL,PRESS,%PRESTAB% !Apply pressure along line (zero at one end, rho*g*Hw at the other)

!Select everything
ALLSEL,ALL


!Apply temperatures as a function of height
*DIM,TEMPTAB,TABLE,5,,,Y
TEMPTAB(1,0)=0,0.25,0.5,0.75,1
TEMPTAB(0,1)=0,130,110,75,35,4
*VOPER,TEMPTAB(1,0),TEMPTAB(1,0),MULT,H
BF,ALL,TEMP,%TEMPTAB%

SOLVE
/POST1

!Create array of resulting displacements
*DIM,DISPS,,ndinqr(0,14),3
*VGET,DISPS(1,1),NODE,1,U,X
*VGET,DISPS(1,2),NODE,1,U,Y

!Fill in USUM values
*DO,i,1,ndinqr(0,14)
        DISPS(i,3)=SQRT(DISPS(i,1)**2+DISPS(i,2)**2)
*ENDDO

*VSCFUN,usum_max,MAX,DISPS(1,3)

!Write displacements to towerdisps.txt
*CFOPEN,towerdisps,txt
*VWRITE,usum_max
('Maximum total displacement = ',F6.4)
*VWRITE
(' ')
*VWRITE
('Nodal Displacements:')
*VWRITE
(' ')
*VWRITE
('Node',2X,'X-Disps',2X,'Y-Disps',4X,'Total')
*VWRITE
('----',2X,'-------',2X,'-------',3X,'------')
*VWRITE,SEQU,DISPS(1,1),DISPS(1,2),DISPS(1,3)
```

```
(F4.0,3F9.4)
*CFCLOSE


!Aesthetic viewing commands not necessary to workshop
!sbctran,u              !Transfer constraints from lines to underlying elements
!sftran            !Transfer pressures from lines to underlying elements
/auto              !Fit model in window
/psf,press,2   !Turn on pressure arrows
/pbc,u,1              !Turn on constraints
/pbf,temp,,1   !Turn on temperature contours
/edge,,1               !Show only element edges so that temperature contours are more
visible
wpstyle         !Turn off workplane display
eplot                !Plot elements
```

Appendix 3: Files Used in Workshops

Several of the workshops use files that the user does not have to create. You can download a ZIP file containing those files from:

www.padtinc.com/apdl_files.zip

The text in the files is also reproduced here in case you are unable to download the files and wish to type them in.

---

bracket6ws.mac

```
!!!!!!!!!!!!!!!!!!!!!!!!!!!!!!!!!!!!
!                                  !
!         bracket6ws.mac           !
!           Written by             !
!         Jeffrey Strain           !
!        November 18, 2003         !
!                                  !
!  This file is to be modified     !
!  to satisfy the objectives of    !
!  Workshop 7 of the ANSYS         !
!  APDL and Customization class.   !
!                                  !
!!!!!!!!!!!!!!!!!!!!!!!!!!!!!!!!!!!!
fini
/clear

!Parameter definitions
Elemtype=92
Eb=29e6
Nub=0.27
CTEb=3e-6
Force=100
Rb=0.1
W=3
D=4
H=4
T=0.25
Rh=1

/PREP7
K,1,0,0,0,
K,2,T,0,0,
K,3,T,H-T,0,
K,4,W,H-T,0,
K,5,W,H,0,
K,6,0,H,0,
L,        1,         6
L,        6,         5
L,        2,         3
L,        3,         4
!*
LFILLT,1,2,Rb+T, ,
!*
LFILLT,3,4,Rb, ,

A,1,2,9,10,4,5,8,7

VEXT,ALL, , ,0,0,D,,,,

KWPAVE,5,17
wprot,0,-90,0
CYL4, , ,Rh, , , , ,-T
```

```
VSBV,       1,        2
!*
ET,1,elemtype
!*
!*
!*
MPTEMP,,,,,,,
MPTEMP,1,0
MPDATA,EX,1,,Eb
MPDATA,PRXY,1,,Nub
MPDATA,ALPX,1,,CTEb
ESIZE,T,0,
MSHAPE,1,3D
MSHKEY,0
!*
VMESH,ALL
!*
FINISH
/SOL
ASEL,S,LOC,Y,0
DA,ALL,ALL,
ALLSEL
ASEL,S,LOC,X,W
NSLA,S,1
!*
*GET,NUMNODE,NODE,,COUNT, , , ,
!*
/GO
F,ALL,FY,-Force/NUMNODE
ALLSEL,ALL
FINISH
```

fastnodearray.mac

```
!fastnodearrays.mac
!Created by Jeff Strain, PADT
!Used to demonstrate speed of vector operations
!over *DO loops
!May also be used as a template

!Create array of selected node numbers
!the fast way

*dim,nodesel,,ndinqr(0,14)
*dim,nodenums,,ndinqr(0,14)
*dim,fastnodes,,ndinqr(0,13)

*vget,nodesel(1),node,1,nsel
*vfill,nodenums(1),ramp,1,1
*vmask,nodesel(1)
*vfun,fastnodes(1),comp,nodenums(1)

*del,nodesel,,nopr
*del,nodenums,,nopr
```

slownodearray.mac

```
!slownodearrays.mac
!Created by Jeff Strain, PADT
!Used to demonstrate slowness of *DO loops
!compared to vector operations
!Don't use this.  Use fastnodearrays.mac
```

```
!Create array of selected node numbers
!the slow way

*get,maxnode,node,0,num,max
*get,nnodes,node,0,count

*dim,slownodes,,nnodes

j=1
*do,i,1,maxnode
*if,nsel(i),eq,1,then
slownodes(j)=i
j=j+1
*endif
*enddo

maxnode=
nnodes=
i=
j=
```

nodewater.mac

```
!Define and activate local cylindrical coordinate system (11) at center of tank
LOCAL,11,1,,H-RT                !Define CS 11
CSYS,11

!Calculate parameters for convenience
RIT=RT-TT                       !Inner radius of tank
ALPHA=90+ASIN((HW-RIT)/RIT)     !Angle between horizontal and intersection of tank and
waterline in CS 11

!Apply varying pressure (between 0 and rho*g*hw) to line
LSEL,S,LOC,X,RIT       !Select all lines along inner radius of tank
LSEL,R,LOC,Y,-90,ASIN((HW-RIT)/RIT)    !Reselect line between bottom of tank and waterline
NSLL,,1
RIT=
ALPHA=
CSYS,0
```

prescoefs.txt

```
Pressure Coefficients vs. Location

X-Loc   Z-Location
0       0       1.2     3
.35     .1      .15     .09
1.145   .3      .4      .5
2.3375  .9      1       .8
3       .5      .75     .45
```

temperatures.txt

```
Applied Temperatures vs. Location

X-Loc   Y-Location
0       0       1       2       3       4
0       600     480     390     300     240
1.8     540     420     360     240     210
```

| 2.55 | 450 | 360 | 270 | 210 | 150 |
| 3 | 300 | 210 | 180 | 120 | 60 |

Printed in Great Britain
by Amazon

46268429R00130